# Tapestry of Voi

GU00891452

*Raised in a Jewish family and married to an Anglican clergyman, Michele Guinness is a freelance journalist. She has worked extensively in radio and television, for two years presenting her own programme on BBC local radio. Most recently she has been the press officer for a children's hospice in Lancashire. Her other books include* Child of the Covenant *and* The Guinness Legend.

# Tapestry of Voices

*Meditations in Celebration
of Women*

MICHELE GUINNESS

TRIANGLE

First published 1993
Triangle
SPCK
Holy Trinity Church
Marylebone Road
London NW1 4DU

British Library Cataloguing in Publication Data

A catalogue record for this book is available from the British Library.

ISBN 0-281-04675-1

Typeset by Pioneer Associates, Perthshire
Printed in Great Britain at
the University Press, Cambridge

# Contents

# Introduction

I am strong. I'm invincible. I am woman.

So says the pop song, and so say women down through the centuries, as they affirm their status alongside men in this world. They may not have fought in a war, but they have fought many other, equally tortuous battles. And sometimes they have won. Sometimes they have lost. But they remain undefeated.

This is a record of the milestones in our struggles, from birth to the grave. The loving, giving and gaining, the hurts, hang-ups and hormones, the breathtaking dexterity with which we juggle countless different jobs and play many different parts, and the exhaustion it causes, are all integral parts of women's pilgrimage. My original idea was to compile a book of meditations specifically for women, but I don't really believe the sexes differ very greatly in the requirements of their spiritual diet. So this is a compilation about women, for women and the men who like them.

But why concentrate on women at all?

First, because there is still a great deal of ambivalence about our spiritual identity. However the structures may appear to change, it is still not easy to be a woman in the Church. Sister Elizabeth Rees, a Roman Catholic pastoral assistant, likened it to being a woodworm, gnawing away at the planks of an archaic institution, until one day the dead wood crumbles and thousands of joyful woodworms lift their praises to the skies!

This compilation is a foretaste. A small chorus of woodworms finds a voice.

Second, women are more in touch with the intricate nuances of body, mind, feeling and spirit, more aware of the cross-currents of experience and spirituality, more conscious of the many undertows in their lives. Men, sadly, have not been nearly as perceptive, or as articulate, about their maleness and its influence on their spirituality. Some Orthodox Jews argue that the very rhythmical nature of a woman's body predisposes her to a natural harmony with the Eternal, revealed in the vast cycles of time and nature. Nevertheless, they thank Him daily that they are not her!

Which brings me to my final reason for an anthology about women. We are different from men. And glad to be. In this compilation we rejoice in our many roles, as daughter, sister, mother, lover, wife, friend, colleague and minister. We explore our distinctively feminine perceptions, smile at our foibles, put our pain to good use, revel in our achievements. We celebrate our femaleness. We are she who God made in His likeness.

# *In the Beginning*

## Chauvinist Creation

Dear Earth,
    Here is man.
        Love,
            God.

P.S. Here is woman.

*Gordon Bailey*

Well perhaps it wasn't quite like that! Even though for many women that is how it may feel. For that rather wry view of creation, written by a man, seems to sum up the subconscious, if not conscious attitude towards women, which has governed the relationships between the sexes for centuries, both outside the Church, and especially within it.

God took from man, not a lung, not a kidney, not a piece of intestine or heart, but a rib, one of many, and therefore an entirely dispensable part of his anatomy, in order to form another human being, like him, yet very different. That rib was a fatal symbol. Within the Judaeo-Christian tradition woman was seen as an inferior version of man, dependent on him for her very existence, coming from him to cater for him in all his physical and emotional needs. That was her only, yet crucial source of power.

The early church fathers bitterly resented and feared that

power. For them Eve was the temptress, she who led man astray, the cause of his downfall, the very gateway to hell itself. If man could only manage to resist her wicked wiles and charm, he would be strong, true and Godlike.

Clearly there is a great danger of misunderstanding the original creation story and its meaning. The early church fathers interpreted it in favour of their own sex. They were not alone. Several writers here take a fresh and inventive look at this key moment in the history of humankind and try to restore some kind of balance.

According to another male poet, Stewart Henderson, woman and man were made to dance together in perfect harmony, in a magnificent ballroom filled with glittering chandeliers. Together they tried to rewrite the movements and the rhythms, and forfeited the waltz. But throughout this collection of meditations and poems, we will see woman listening out for the strains of that original tune, tapping her feet, trying out a few steps, as she tries to rediscover 'the leader, thinker, mother' God made, as she struggles to regain the paradise, the 'Godlikeness' that was lost.

*HILARY McDOWELL is a dramatist, journalist, poet, counsellor and psychologist. At present Director of the Multi-Media Workshop in Belfast, she is also a deaconess in the Presbyterian Church of Ireland, exercising a ministry of outreach and reconciliation within all the denominations through drama, art and music.*

*Disabled from birth seven times over, she represents Northern Ireland on the European Community Commission for Arts and Disability. As the first contributor to this compilation, she also represents the highest qualities of faithfulness and determination which were potentially moulded into the woman God made.*

## The Making of Eve

Grubbing in the dust
He found the mud a trifle squelchy
Found the ribs a little brittle
Found the rib that needed taking
For the mould that needed breaking
Re-cycled, not forsaken
For the she that he was making.

Wading through the mud
He found the clay a little cracked
Found the dirt a little grubby
Found the dirt that grows the earth-life
Placed the seed of his own mirth life
Re-united joy with sorrow
For the she he deemed was worth life.

Dancing to the sea
He found the light would sparkle radiant
Found the waves would flow succinctly
Found an ebb tide just her colour
For a leader, thinker, mother
Uniquely stamped in his image
To present her to the other.

Weeping by the pool
He found her eyes reflecting distance
Found the pain that hid the future
Found the pain that pierced him also
For how sword from sickle grows
Lies not within the earth plan
Such knowledge only reptile shows.

Standing by the tree
He found the glimpse into her future
Found the tears she'd weep beside him
Found the wood to carve their death stake
For the she he'd made for God's sake
Heart pierced and womb rekindled
Soon would kindle him for earth's sake.

Grubbing in the dust
He found the mud a trifle squelchy
Found the hearts a little brittle
Found the hearts that needed taking
For the world that needed making
Re-born not unforgiven
Those who bear the name of women.

*Hilary McDowell*

*How different would the creation story have been if it had been written by a woman? This is what the following piece sets out to explore, and while purists might question its theological acceptability, it nonetheless carries its own particular challenge. It was written during the Gulf War of 1991.*

### Eve's Story

Well you know what men are like
always writing history instead of her story
but what actually happened was
that we were sitting in the cool of the day
chatting about fruit
and God said she could never decide
whether
raspberries or strawberries tasted best

6

and the fox said he preferred sour grapes
but the vixen disagreed
and Adam said he'd like to try the fruit of
the tree
of knowledge of good and evil
and God said she wouldn't advise it
because
it could cause delusions but of course
she wasn't going to make any rules
and it was up to Adam.

He was a little worried about the delusions
because he always prides himself on his
reason
but I suppose it niggled away at him and
anyway he thinks his reason can
override any delusions
and so one day he picked one of the fruits
and said to me Eve
you go and count all the animals
and get the supper
and tidy yourself up a bit
and don't forget to feed the snake
and I'll sit and eat this fruit.

So I went down to look at the water lilies
until the cool of the day
and as I was wandering back with God
talking with the lily-feathered swans
Adam rushed up to us and shouted
O thou art the lord my god
and thou art a jealous god
and God replied
I am neither a lord nor jealous
but Adam took no notice
and he raved on.

It's all Eve's fault
because she fed not the snake
and the snake beguiled me
and I did eat of the fruit
whereof thou toldest me
that I should not eat
and I am undone
and God said don't worry about it
and stop listening to your superego.

But Adam raged
alas we were naked
let us sew garments of fig leaves
we are accurst and thy sorrow Eve
will be greatly multiplied
when thou bringest forth children in pain
and the ground is cursed for our sake
and we shall till it
thorns and thistles also shall it bring forth
and in the sweat of our faces shall we eat
bread
until we return as dust to the ground
for we are driven out of Eden
and he took my arm and dragged me through a gateway
and God said sadly that
she wouldn't make any rules
and that it was up to us.

Somehow there were these giant
thistles
and when I went back to look for the gate
I couldn't find it
but I didn't have much time
what with tilling and baking and babies
and all that

though it was a little easier
when Adam invented machinery
except of course that all is
seared with trade bleared smeared with toil
and even if you might catch a glimpse of
the gate
it's lost now in the burning oil fields
and the smoke of Adam's delusions.

*Born and brought up in Coventry, VERONICA ZUNDEL was born to Austrian parents. Her father was Jewish. For several years she worked and wrote for the Christian current affairs magazine,* Third Way, *and also had a regular column in* Christian Woman, *which won a national award. She has written extensively on the role of women in the Church, dating, and being single. In 1989, when she was 36, she married Ed Sirett.*

*In the poem 'Deception' she plays with a favourite idea: that Eve's mistake was to undervalue herself. What the tempter offered her – Godlikeness – she already had.*

## Deception

In Eden's sun the woman basks,
she works, plays, loves as each day asks
and knows not she is God's mirror and sign;
till, curving elegant his tail,
the serpent (who is surely male)
insinuates a lack of the divine.

'To be like God' – a worthy goal
for any self-improving soul,
an offer she, or man, can scarce disdain.
Poor Eve! Why won't she realize
right now she's able, strong and wise
with nothing but the choice of good to gain?

Yet still the priests perpetuate
the lie that led to Eden's gate
and raised the fiery sword our bliss to bar:
still women make the same mistake
and bow to some religious snake
who tells us we are not the gods we are.

*Veronica Zundel*

*STEWART HENDERSON is that rare commodity in the Church and even outside the Church – a successful poet. He has published five collections of poetry and a sixth is due out soon. His work can even be found in various set GCSE anthologies. He often performs his work alongside his wife, Carol, on tour in roadshows. His monthly interview series, 'On the Receiving End' at The Nave in Uxbridge, has included guests such as Germaine Greer, Esther Rantzen, Stephen Fry and Anita Roddick.*

*I have included several of his poems in this collection, because he manages to capture, in a way few other male poets do, the wistfulness women often feel about their relationships with men. In fact the battle between the sexes is a major theme in his 'Counter-Balance' roadshow.*

## Counter-Balance

This is how it was
before I dipped canaries in sunlight
and gave the water buffalo its rolling stroll
before the dolphin had told its first joke
not even the lion had yet leaped from his lair
This was how it was;
with my Perfect Partners
We laid out the dance floor
opened up the ballroom of creation
hung planets as lanterns
and stars for concealed lighting.
Our choreography lasted light years
and our joy far longer.
Then We constructed a dressing-room
We called it 'Earth'
It was pure, and it shone
And it smelled like Me.
In time, I employed a couple of attendants
and invited them
to come and make up a fivesome.
They were both so beautiful
But they refused
and started to make up their own
disjointed steps
as the dressing-room faded into shadow.
And so I wrote My grief
Over everything I had made
and pined for my two attendants.
One of my perfect Partners
even entered the dressing-room
to invite them once again
to join Our unblemished company

11

They sent Him back
bloodied, pummelled, gored.
They were even going to break His legs
They thought that would stop Him dancing.
But that I would not allow
For it was His dancing
His pleading arabesque
that turned away My wrath
and lit up the deep darkness.

*Stewart Henderson*

# *Girls*

Within the Jewish community giving birth to a son is a sign of God's special blessing, celebrated by all the family on the eighth day in a service known as the 'brith', the circumcision or 'covenant' ceremony. A son bears and continues the family name, say the special memorial prayers for a deceased father and grandfather in the Synagogue, inherits the religious responsibilities and traditions. But the actual religious and racial identity is passed on through the woman. A group of Liberal Jewish women in America are now designing a special ceremony of thanksgiving for a girlchild.

There is something infinitely precious about having a daughter. Mine, from the moment she was born, drew from me reserves of tenderness, protectiveness and fight I never knew I possessed. I wanted to change the world overnight, to make it a safer, easier, better place for this miniature woman, this receptacle of all my dreams and aspirations, this extension of myself.

'Thank heavens for little girls.' And they are not just their potential as women. With pigtails and pony tails, in jeans and party dresses, climbing trees, reading books, sucking gob-stoppers and turning cartwheels, making friends and breaking friends, they bring their special charm into the world, a delight in detail, a tenderness in relationship, a sensitivity to joy and sorrow and spiritual truth; the many attributes which make them different from little boys. They can have, as Hilary McDowell's experience shows, a longing to serve God and be his minister from a very early age.

Advice to mothers on how to bring up their daughters has always been plentiful. 'Lock them up', 'Don't put them on the stage'; they seem to amount to a series of negatives. Small wonder that bringing a girlchild into the world seems a rather frightening business. And now, with more sexual license than ever, with the spectre of AIDS, with so many new, exciting opportunities for women, as well as the hazards which lie hidden in wait in the potential minefields they have to manoeuvre, what can we give our girls to help them through the confusing, glorious process of growing into womanhood, so that, happy, whole and free, they fulfil their birthright, and become the ministers God intends them to be?

## The Girlchild

I bear you quickly,
Pain curbed.
Scarce believing
The miracle of speed
From wet, dark root
Through womb's gates
To life's gasp.
Feel your quick descent,
Head round as elemental Earth:
Give all my strength
To body's ruthless call.
See your head appear,
Hold my breath for
Last long thrusting heave
Then tiny body's rush.
You are born.
A girlchild.

*Jenny Cooke*

*EVANGELINE PATERSON was born in Limavady in Northern Ireland and lived in Dublin until she married an Englishman, a lecturer in geography. She has spent her time moving round with him to different universities -- Cambridge, St Andrews and Leicester – writing poetry, and bringing up three children. Watching them leave home was a major trauma in her life, and letting go of them a powerful theme in her poetry.*

*For years Evangeline has been deeply committed to the revival of the arts amongst evangelical Christians. Her two major collections of poems are* Bringing the Water Hyacinth to Africa *and* Lucifer at the Fair, *and though she has won prizes for her poems, including a Cheltenham Festival Prize, is only now receiving the recognition in the Church which her work deserves.*

*For ten years she edited a magazine* Other Poetry *and now, though officially 'retired', works for* Stand *magazine in Newcastle-upon-Tyne.*


## Advice to Daughters

Beware the men who seek
the soft and changing tone
of youth upon the cheek
and overlook the bleak
white armature of bone.

He is a fool who loves
only the dimpled face.
It is the bone that moves
ungainly, or with grace
to fill a singing space.

And time will come and hone
his sharp and eager beak
upon the flesh alone,
and then the bone will speak.

*Evangeline Paterson*

*In this poem VERONICA ZUNDEL, who married quite late in life,
manages to capture the problems many single young women
face in their search for the ideal relationship, and their
frustrations with Christian men!*

## Suppose Boaz

Suppose Boaz
hadn't been honourable.
Suppose he had, finding
at his feet a warm and
willing woman, sleepily
reached out and taken what
any man today (they say)
would.

Suppose in blank and grainy
morning light, he'd seen
the space impressed where she
had been, and yawned
luxurious, wondering
who she was, but not much
taxing curiosity – gifts should be
accepted where they fall, and never
tainted with rue or ruth.

16

Or say he'd been
worse, an evangelical Christian
what then, in dangerous dark brought close against
such vulnerable, physical
daring femaleness? Oh, but he'd surely
shrink in terror at the smirching of
his guarded virtue: what prim and pious
flight he'd take!

Dear Ruth, you were luckier than
I: he talked to you.
If men had such courage now.

*Veronica Zundel*

*In the Far East women are beginning to express loudly and clearly the frustrations they feel about their position in society. The translator of the next piece, MUKTI BARTON, is an Indian Bengali, now married to an Anglican clergyman and living in the south of England. For ten years she lived in Bangladesh where she founded Netritto Proshikkhon Kendro, an ecumenical training centre for women, which struggled for the kind of justice required by Christian theology.*

*Bangladeshi women are victims of a very strong patriarchal structure, strengthened by a misinterpretation of Islam. Lack of education and poverty compound their problems. Girls fortunate to be born into homes where they receive a good education still struggle with insecurity, exploitation and an inability to fulfil their true promise and potential, as this piece, written by an Asian Christian from Bangladesh, shows.*

## For You are a Woman

Woman,
the cry with which at your birth you tell
'Here I am'
that cry today fills people with fear,
for you are a woman.

You will grow a little, learn to walk and run,
be everybody's darling,
and from that moment you are no more secure
for you are a woman.

Grown up you'll go to school and college.
Your mother stands waiting at the door,
Who knows if you will return unharmed
for you are a woman.

When they see you, boys will whistle
One throws stones,
another acid:
you are never safe
for you are a woman.

Once married, your husband's puppet,
to play as he pleases,
Your own desires will never come first:
but when there is blame to bear
it will fall on you only –
the slightest thing a ground for divorce
for you are a woman.

So beware!
Do not be so helpless
that your mouth stays shut.
Be the voice of protest
take for yourself the nights that are yours.
Not just as a woman are you to live
But as a full human being.

*Zeemat Ahmed*
*Translated by Mukti Barton*

## The Gospel According to Abby

I never cease to be impressed by the amount of worldly wisdom which pours from the lips of children. And I must confess, sexist though it may be, that I find little girls do have the knack of articulating their perceptions of life in a particularly fascinating way.

My little Abby, at eight, sometimes had the insights of an eighty-year-old. I shall never forget the day she greeted me when I came in from work in a state of high excitement. Had I heard about the accident at school?

I hadn't.

'Well', she said and launched into her story with relish.

I half listened, while the other half of me planned the tea. Apparently Abby's friend Sarah had been propelling herself around the playground like a miniature torpedo, when along came Mark Higginbotham playing at torpedoes in the opposite direction. Their heads met and Helena, who had witnessed the disaster, had rushed across the playground to tell Abby and her friend Andrea that Sarah was pouring with blood from an enormous gash across one eyebrow.

19

'Hmmph', Andrea had said, 'Don't bother telling me, she's not my friend any more.'

Abby was shocked at her friend's callousness, until Andrea's face crumpled and the little girl broke into an enormous howl.

'Andrea, whatever's the matter?' Abby asked.

'It's all my fault for breaking friends with Sarah. If she'd been my friend she'd have been playing here with me.'

At that point Helena burst into tears too. 'No, it's my fault. I persuaded her to play torpedoes.'

They were quickly joined by several other little girls who all began to cry as well, saying it was their fault. No it wasn't, it was Andrea's fault. No, it was Helena's fault. Then they all agreed it was Mark Higginbotham's fault, since he was a boy, and felt much better.

Abby rattled on. 'I didn't cry. I said, "What a nonsense!"'

It was at that point that she suddenly had my full attention.

'What did you say?' I asked her.

She repeated confidently, 'I said, "What a nonsense!" Well, it was no one's fault, was it? It's silly to look for someone to blame. Accidents happen.'

Abby was right. How we love to look for someone to blame. Politicians thrive on it. People sue and make a fortune out of it. The newspapers sell on it. The legal profession make a field day out of it. Hunt the scapegoat! And what a nonsense it is. Could it be that like Andrea and Helena, shifting blame is one way of coping with our own guilty feelings? What a relief it is to find someone who has done something worse than I. It makes me feel much better about the mistakes I've made.

We all make mistakes, on a minor or very major scale. The greater the mistake the greater the burden of guilt, but Jesus singled out guilty people for compassion not blame. That's why he became the greatest scapegoat of all time.

May adults everywhere hearken to the gospel according to a little girl.

*Michele Guinness*

8 years old and called to the ministry
8 years old and not a day more
Go now Lord, let me start right now
I have love to give, I have perfume to pour.
Wait, my child
There's no hurry, my love
Your feet tread on an icy floor.
There's a crying and aching and hurting to do
There's a dying to do, and more.

Go now Lord, let me go right now
To the sea where the fishes are caught
I will swim and dive and fight the waves
Till the nets to the shore are brought.
Wait, my child, there is time still
For the water's plunge
There is time for the spray and the surf
For the spume and the rocks and the whale's tooth
To measure and prove your worth.

Let me love you first, my little one
Let me love and caress and hold
For there's time to come
In the bitter storms
When you'll lift your arms to the cold.

Let me come now, let me come Lord
Now that the dying is here.
Let me rest in your arms
And lie in your love
Till I feel your hope vanquish all fear.
Come now, my child, for now's the time
Now's the time when I'm here.

*Hilary McDowell*

21

# A Woman's Love

So critical is the Church of the trivializing of love in contemporary society that it has tended to undervalue romance altogether, conveying the idea that it is at best a very poor gateway into the more meaningful area of commitment, at worst a superficial, transient, adolescent aberration.

Yet those who fall in love, and it can happen in youth or old age, not only know that the lyrics of the pop songs are true, but they can also find spiritual enrichment in their experience. And though there may be immense pain involved in loving they would not, says Ellen Wilkie, after her romance was all over, 'choose to leave the cup standing', for, as the 67-year-old Henry Grattan Guinness puts it, bowled over by the charms of a woman more than forty years his junior, 'heaven is found in the bosom of love'.

Loving is as close to perfection as we shall ever come in this life, for it provides an unparalleled opportunity to glimpse the twinkle in God's eye.

*ELLEN WILKIE (1958–89) was one of the few women ever to have the genetically-inherited wasting disease, Duschenne Muscular Dystrophy. Though not expected to survive into her twenties, she defied all the odds by living a full and active thirty-one years. In that time she became an actress, TV presenter and poet. She had no time for anyone who passed*

23

*her over because she was confined to a wheelchair, and a
woman. She stalwartly refused to blame God for her condition
or submit to the limitations of her body and packed more into
her thirty-one years than most people do in a lifetime. 'When I
take a retrospective glance and compare my deepest desires
with what I have done in reality I sit back in amazement, as if I
am looking at the life of another person. I never expected my
cup to be filled, but its running over.'*

*She was particularly glad that despite being physically
handicapped there had been the chance to love. Her one long-
term romance however was a bitter-sweet affair, making her
long for the chance to be an equal among equals. Living
together in water, she says, would have given her that chance.*

### Walking on Water

only ask me to live with you in water
or on the moon
and I'll be your dancing partner all year long
queen of my once-a-week domain
I relive my previous walking
toe-heel, toe-heel, toe-heel
all the blissful width of the pool
a liquid life brings me alive
with balletic sweeps
swinging in the watery freedom
which air denies
graceful control of my weekly gift

only meet me in the water
where I'm granted equal footing
I can walk to you with life, life, life
self-propelled limbs feel female
as strength surges to support
where outside my water-world
gravity lets me down
only ask me to live with you in water

*Ellen Wilkie*

*Love at first sight still provokes poetry! PAM CAVENDISH was only nineteen when she met the man she was to marry. She wrote this poem two days later, recalling how the gathering storm which accompanied her journey home on the train mirrored exactly the growing storm within. 'We were both at a party; didn't know each other and had hardly spoken, but there was such an attraction. Then he kissed me. What a kiss, it awoke something in me!'*

*Pam has worked as an editor at the national office of Relate in Rugby. As well as being a freelance writer, she now works in public relations for the Coventry Health Authority. She and her husband are members of the Coventry Christian Fellowship.*

### After the First Kiss

Distant storm beginning to grow,
Seeming, moving, ominously slow.
Surging up in me
With increasing clouds,
Encroaching intensity; half allowed.

Strong and heavy, weighted low,
But from under its oppression there begins to flow;
All-rising, soon overwhelmed,
By writhing waters and walls of wind
Flows and closes and holds and moulds
All it touches and all it feels,
My impossible no to the daring air.
Freeing care.
Releases and thrills
An upturned face to feel rain that spills
Onto moistened eyes and through my sighs, hear,
'Kiss me in the rain before you go.'

*Pam Cavendish*

*Whether the woman is nineteen or a little more mature,
whether the object of her passion is seventeen, or nearly
seventy, as in this case, a kiss can be the signal for love to
assault its victim with unanticipated violence.*

*GRACE HURDITCH GUINNESS (1878–1967) thought she was
a confirmed spinster when she met the famous preacher and
Bible teacher, Henry Grattan Guinness in 1903. He was 67, a
widower and lonely. He had been praying for God to send him
a wife for some time, and had dreamed, in 1900, of a woman
who had sat on his knee – and kissed him – 'with a bright
smile, her own act'.*

*This is how Grace described their meeting three years later
to her sister who was a missionary in Africa.*

Well, his magnificent presence appealed to me very strongly,
his clean-shaven face and white hair brushed back off that
great forehead of his. He tells me that his first impressions of

me were 'What a sweet girl', and from that moment we felt most strongly drawn to each other. He watched me a great deal at lunch. Harvey Harte was sitting next to me and noticed it. Edith Greenhill sat at the head, and of course she noticed it.

Well after lunch we had tea as usual, and everyone went out but the Doctor and me, and strange to say I did not feel in the least afraid of him as the great Dr Guinness, as everyone else seemed to be. And then he took my hand and asked me a little about myself and what I was doing here, after which he gave me a kiss – such a kiss – and I loved him and felt I never wanted to leave him, but never thought for a moment that he would care for me like that. Such a thought never crossed my mind. I only knew that it was an exquisite day to be with him then and the future never occurred to me.

. . . Then, Friday night, darling, he asked me to come and have a talk with him in the office, and he drew me to him and told me how he loved me right from the first, and how for five years he had prayed God to bring him this love, which I had awakened in him, love, he tells me such as he has never known before.

*Grace Hurditch Guinness*

*And after Grace had sat on his knee that Friday evening,*
*which she did, spontaneously, Henry poured out his thanks to*
*God in a poem which celebrates the rapture a woman's love*
*can bring, even to a man of more mature years!*

She has come to my arms, she has come to my heart.
And the dream of my soul is fulfilled,
And the love that unites us shall never depart,
Nor the love that our union has willed.

O thanks to the Giver, O thanks for the gift,
From the gift to the Giver we turn;
From the bliss he bestows to himself we uplift
The hearts which with gratitude burn.

There is heaven below, there is heaven above,
And they answer like ocean and sky;
For heaven is found in the bosom of love,
In spirit to spirit made nigh.

*Henry Grattan Guinness*

*ELLEN WILKIE graphically captures here the physical pain of parting forever when loving is finished. Yet with God no experience, however painful, is ever wasted. It brings its own particular comfort. It leaves its special mark.*

## Ex

Funny to think you're
just another 'ex' to add to the list
when you're anything but
'just another ex to add to the list'
Textured visions of our past holding-hand happiness
torment me with their beautiful simplicity
but like a bitter sweet draught
I could not choose to leave the cup standing
or let my lips stay dry

Our lives were intertwined
on the verge of the sacred vows
unpicking the twine
takes more than time
don't pull so fast
that I spin in dizzy turns
that you suffer rope burns
We still have skin grafts
yours to mine
mine to yours
some will stay
and it should remain that way
and it shall remain that way.

*Ellen Wilkie*

# Marriage

Do you ever think how kind it was of God to make such a relationship a HOLY one, so that his own children may realise more bliss in it than in any other?

*Catherine Booth*

Any married woman who has ever tried her hand at writing, writes at some time or another about marriage. For of all her relationships it affects woman the most profoundly, whether for good or ill.

'Marriage', said the Scottish preacher Peter Marshall, who became chaplain to the United States Senate, was 'God's greatest gift to man'. It can potentially, as William and Catherine Booth discovered, be an ongoing taste of heaven, a continuation of the rapture first experienced in the heady, early days of romantic love. Human beings, as many of these pieces portray, can be an immense source of strength and support to each other. Men can be the means whereby their wives are released to fulfil their highest potential. A wife can turn a vulnerable, insecure husband into a giant of a man.

On the other hand, marriage can be hell, a cage in which woman feels stifled, restricted, diminished, so that she is forced ultimately to break free in some way in order to find herself. During a funeral visit my husband was once asked by the bereaved widow whether he thought she would ever see her deceased husband again. Thinking that like many women

31

she needed the comfort of knowing they would meet again, he took great care with his words. She might, he said, see him again. But in heaven there appeared to be no such institution as marriage. 'Thank God,' she said with a sigh of relief, 'I've had enough of him down here.'

But even though marriage confronts us with our own unresolved inner conflict and turmoil, as Joyce Huggett reveals when she describes her jealousy of the secretary, even though love be an immensely 'precarious thing', according to the poet Stewart Henderson, the 'tenacious weeds' Jenny Cooke speaks of can be slowly and painfully pulled, when there is the will and commitment to do so. But the challenge of the relationship, the hard work, the struggle to find independence and individuality in togetherness, never comes to an end, for 'untouched land rolls on joyously to the horizon'.

*CATHERINE BOOTH (1829–90) with her husband, William, left the Methodist Church in 1865 to found 'The Christian Mission', which later became the Salvation Army. Their love story is as enchanting, if not more so, than any romantic novel. Their lifelong devotion to each other played no small part in their success in establishing the new denomination.*

*Encouraged by her husband, Catherine was one of the few women of her time to take the pulpit and preach. As he was only too well aware, she was a powerful and moving preacher, and he was never a man to worry about being overshadowed when God's work was to be done.*

*Perhaps if like Catherine Booth women today took the time to work out a code of essentials for the man of their choice, there might be many more successful relationships. But whether we have any right to expect God to deliver our blueprint with even the favoured Christian name is a matter for conjecture!*

## On Choosing a Husband

As quite a young girl I made up my mind. He must be a sincere Christian; not a nominal one or a mere church member, but truly converted to God. I resolved that he should be a man of sense. I knew that I could never respect a fool, or one much weaker mentally than myself.

The third essential consisted of oneness of views and tastes, any ideas of lordship or ownership being lost in love. There can be no doubt that Jesus Christ intended, by making love the law of marriage, to restore woman to the position God intended her to occupy. Of course there must be mutual yielding whenever there is proper love, because it is a pleasure and a joy to yield our own wills to those for whom we have real affection, whenever it can be done with an approving conscience.

Neither party should attempt to force an alliance where there exists a physical repugnance. Natural instinct in this respect is usually too strong for reason, and asserts itself in after life in such a way so as to make both supremely miserable.

Another resolution that I made was that I would never marry a man who was not a total abstainer, and this from conviction, and not merely to gratify me.

Besides these things, which I looked upon as being absolutely essential, I had, like most people, certain preferences. The first was that the object of my choice should be a minister, for I felt I could be most useful to God as a minister's wife. Then I very much desired that he should be dark and tall, and had a special liking for the name, 'William'. Singularly enough, in adhering to my essentials, my fancies were also gratified.

*Catherine Booth*

*'Every married man has a motive for murder', claims crime writer Ruth Rendell's Inspector Wexford. But what many married men fail to realize, and this poem written by a man so clearly conveys, is that women may well be prone to her own frustrations when confronted with the great masculine mystique.*

## A Wife Meditates on her Beloved From the Bathroom

He always leaves the toilet seat up
and sometimes he's splashed
It must have been a woman
who invented the pedestal mat
An expression of ironic protest
that is now essential furnishing
On waking, he makes the most bizarre noises
He sounds like a beached walrus belching
and blowing an off-key trumpet
whilst revving up a Harley Davidson
Why is this so?
Why are there bristles in the basin?
And the untidiness
What does one sock on top of the ottoman mean?
Do you take this hurricane to be your
lawful wedded husband?
Is this him being himself?
Do I feel disillusioned?
Do I feel resentful and used?
Could he cope if I screamed at him?
Can any man ever take failure?
Am I nagging or am I pleading
for the real him to be him
and hold the real me?

Why can't he be vulnerable yet strong
at the same time?
Precarious thing, love.

*Stewart Henderson*

## 'Let There Be Spaces in Your Togetherness'

Then Almitra spoke again and said, And what of Marriage, master? And he answered saying:

You were born together, and together you shall be for
   evermore.
You shall be together when the white wings of death
   scatter your days.
Aye, you shall be together even in the silent memory of
   God.
But let there be spaces in your togetherness.
And let the winds of the heavens dance between you.

Love one another, but make not a bond of love:
Let it rather be a moving sea between the shores of your
   souls.
Fill each other's cup but drink not from one cup.
Give one another of your bread but eat not from the same
   loaf.
Sing and dance together and be joyous, but let each one of
   you be alone,
Even as the strings of a lute are alone though they quiver
   with the same music.

Give your hearts, but not into each other's keeping.
For only the Hand of life can contain your hearts.
And stand together yet not too near together:
For the pillars of the temple stand apart,
And the oak tree and the cypress grow not in each other's
shadow.

*Kahlil Gibran*

*ROSE SEAL grew up in a West Yorkshire mining town, where her father worked at one of the local pits. Women in these small communities were expected to play a fairly traditional role. Only in the last few years have they begun to find their wings. After the miners' strike of 1985, Relate was inundated with requests for marriage counselling from women who had discovered their ability to work, fight and feed their families. Many found themselves for the first time and had no intention of climbing back into the cage once their men went back to work.*

*For many couples new attitudes to the role of women have caused a great deal of soul-searching and pain. Where both parties allow for change and growth, a marriage can be strengthened and enriched. But a relationship cast in a concrete mould cannot survive the chiselling determination of a wife who wants to be herself.*

## When Marriage Becomes a Cage

It's not that she really wanted to do it, not deep down. But it had to be, the final attempt to prise open that clam shell called emotion, barnacled shut by generations of male pride and

36

deep-rooted indifference. The years of not knowing what to do had vanished. Today Steve's wife would cease to be.

She went through the usual morning rituals, peanut butter sandwiches in plastic bags, feeding the cat, the doorstep kissing, team talks and cheery shouts of goodbye. Look world, have your last gawp at this normal family.

Wearing her fragile 'take care' sticker for the last time, the door finally shut, Steve's wife went into abnormal mode. She dragged the case from underneath the bed and packed it with finality. No extra time, no replays, no substitution. The dress he said she looked like mutton dressed as lamb in. Best underwear he'd bought her, but never noticed.

'Wives, submit yourselves to your husbands . . .' The thought aimed a low punch, but Steve's wife had been expecting it, and ducked, reading the conditions of her single ticket. In the bathroom mirror she examined her reflection, but saw no butterfly wings. 'Wives, submit yourselves to your husbands.' Well-meaning advice, but she left it like the squeezed-dry toothpaste tube on the sink, wishing all the same that it hadn't found a vulnerable spot, which itched.

Photographs in the hall oozed reasons to stay. Steve's wife stared at them and they stared back, cling-filmed to the past like a Barbra Streisand song.

Buttoning her good wool coat she paused to stroke a purr of approval from the cat. She slammed the door behind her, posted the keys through the letter-box and Linda Mary Jackson left the pitch and ran to catch the 9.30 train.

*Rose Seal*

*JOYCE HUGGETT is a prolific writer. She has written several books concentrating on the subject of courtship and marriage, along with many others, including* Listening to God, *and*

Listening to Others, *which have grown out of her experience as a counsellor and spiritual director. She and her husband, David, have left St Nicholas' Church in Nottingham, where he was the rector for many years, to have a more itinerant, international ministry.*

## The Spectre of the Other Woman

Because the work in the church was growing, David and I agreed that his need for secretarial help was urgent. We prayed that God would bring across our path someone with secretarial skills who could relieve him of some of the administrative pressures. Within weeks a young vivacious American girl joined the church . . . I discovered that she was a qualified secretary and that she was job-hunting. I liked her. When I went home I told David about her. A few weeks later she took on the thankless task of setting up the church office.

She had been working with us for only a few weeks when I began to behave in an irrational and unreasonable way. Instead of viewing her presence as an answer to prayer, I resented it. Instead of liking her and welcoming the help she gave in answering the telephone and doorbell, I felt irritated by her presence, which now seemed more like an intrusion than a help. And worse, when she and David worked together in his study I found myself hurting inside in rather the same way as I imagine a person who has been stabbed in the chest must feel.

At first I assumed that this was the jealousy any wife might feel if her husband is working closely alongside an attractive impressionable young woman. So I gave myself a firm ticking off, confessed my 'sin' to God and expected the situation to change. It did change. It grew worse. And worse. And worse.

It was not that I did not trust David's moral integrity. I did. I knew he was trustworthy. But that belief did nothing to temper the irrationality of the panic which seemed to sweep over me whenever he and the secretary were alone together . . .

This went on for months before my study of the ministry of inner healing, or the healing of the memories as it is sometimes called, brought me hope and also persuaded me to take action . . .

The hope in me gave rise to a prayer that Jesus would shine his searchlight into the cellar of my life and expose anything there which was stunting my growth . . . As though in answer to that prayer, I woke up next morning with three distinct childhood memories playing on the video of my mind.

The three memories seemed to be a variation on one theme. Rejection. Or more accurately, perceived rejection. The most painful one was of myself lying in my child-size bed in the corner of my parents' bedroom in Roberts Road. I was burying my head under the blankets while they made love, tears were stinging my eyes but I was fighting them lest I should let out the sobs of loneliness I wanted to cry. I scarcely dared breathe because my mind was telling me that I should not be there. I was intruding. So I lay like a whimpering puppy, too frightened to let out its yelp. I felt desolate.

These feelings intensified if I was still awake when my parents came to bed. On such occasions my mother would talk to me until I was drowsy and drifting off to sleep. Except when she and my father planned to make love. Then she would pretend to have a headache, tell me not to talk tonight, that she was rolling over to go to sleep. A few minutes later I would hear them whispering and kissing and fondling one another and I would feel confused, unwanted, unhappy, abandoned. Pushed out . . .

In my imagination I returned to my bedroom in Roberts Road and as I lay in the bed in my corner, I could feel the blankets and hear the muffled sounds from my parents' bed. I was hurting now just as I had hurt as I lay in that room listening to sounds I should have been protected from. And I cried to God to reach down and rescue me. As I prayed in this way, I plucked up courage to peep out of the blankets and I saw that a screen was now dividing my bed from my parents'. The screen, I noticed, was decorated with angels whose wings stretched almost to the ceiling and touched, giving me the privacy I needed. As I examined the screen those angels seemed to come alive, forming a partition which separated my corner from the rest of the room. And with their presence came the reassuring promise: 'He shall give his angels charge over you to protect you in all your ways.'

I was so convinced that this lay at the root of my irrational behaviour that I expected that once this memory had been touched by God I would change overnight and become warm and loving and outgoing to David's secretary. But, alas, I was to discover that the healing of the memories is not a short cut to maturity, or a formula for finding instant freedom. No. It can be a vital and significant start. But it is only a start to a process which may take months or even years to complete. God, after all, is not in a hurry. He is looking for perfection, not quick results.

*Joyce Huggett*


## Alternative Adultery

I'm up here sobbing. And why? Because the telly's on! Can a man be unfaithful to his wife with a machine? It certainly feels like it. Tonight is our only night in together this week and there's so much to talk about. But he's chosen to spend it with something else.

She never asks awkward questions, demands conversation or expects a response. She's entertaining and intelligent, can make him laugh, can make him cry. She never ages. I can't

40

think why I give her lodging space. We are no longer 'just the two of us'. We are the eternal triangle. And I am the gooseberry.

I'm shut out. And I feel angry. Worse still, when I'm ignored I stomp off. So here I am, sitting upstairs crying.

Please God, tonight, let me time it right, and persuade him to reach for the off-button after the news and weather.

*Pam Cavendish*

*And yet there is an immense sense of satisfaction when the effort this special relationship requires appears to be paying off. JENNY COOKE and her husband have had their fair share of weathering crises together, for they have twice been forced to cope with redundancy and the financial difficulties, worry and sense of loss that can cause.*

*Jenny has written five books, including* The Cross Behind Bars *and* Upon This Rock, *and is now working full time, running a special unit for several hearing-impaired children, attached to a local primary school. This is communication at the other end of the spectrum.*

## The Marriage

Together we survey our land:
A farmstead built,
The nearby fields neatly furrowed,
Faintly green.

Remember the winter toil:
The frozen hands,
Clods of unyielding earth,
Tenacious weeds.

Know the land at last
Is broken to our will.
Tamed by an agony of work
Not possibility.

So we stand quiet.
Then, jerked with surprise, see
There is yet untouched land
Rolling joyously to the horizon.

And beyond.

*Jenny Cooke*

*As time passes, the relationship changes. Sadly, in some cases, the wife may find she has become the mother. MARGERY KEMPE (1373–1438), though she lived so long ago, might have been a contemporary carer. Born in Norfolk in 1393, she married John Kempe and had fourteen children, before she set off on a series of pilgrimages to Italy and the Holy Land and recorded her experiences in* The Book of Margery Kempe. *But her freedom to travel and write, her time for quiet contemplation, was severely curtailed when her husband became totally dependent upon her. Her means of coping with her situation was by seeing it as a punishment for the sexual pleasure she had enjoyed with her husband in the past. Women today, more enlightened about the God-given expression of their sexuality in marriage, might perhaps rather see it as part of the cost of lifelong, loving commitment.*

## When a Wife Becomes a Carer

Then she took her husband home with her and looked after him for as long as he lived. And she worked very hard for in his last days he turned childish again and lost touch. So he could not control his bowels and use a seat, or else he would not, but like a child he voided in his linen at the fire or at the table, wherever he was sitting; he spared no place. And therefore she had much more work washing and wringing and much more expense in drying, and she was kept to a great extent from contemplation. Many times she would have resented her work, except she remembered the many delectable thoughts, fleshly lust and inordinate love she had for him in her youth. And therefore she was glad to be punished with the same person and she took it more easily and served him and helped him, she thought, as she might have done Christ himself.

*from* The Book of Margery Kempe,
*translated by Susan Dickman*

*WILLIAM BOOTH, founder of the Salvation Army, wrote this sermon for his wife's funeral. It must surely be the most moving tribute to a woman, if not love poem, ever written.*

## When the End Comes

If you had a tree . . . under your window, which for forty years had been your shadow from the burning sun, whose flowers had been the adornment and beauty of your life, whose fruit had been almost the very stay of your existence . . .

If you had had a servant who, for all this long time, had served you without fee or reward, who had ministered, for very love, to your health and comfort . . .

If you had had a counsellor who in hours – continually occurring – of perplexity and amazement, had ever advised you . . .

If you had had a friend who had understood your very nature, the rise and fall of your feelings, the bent of your thoughts, and the purpose of your existence; a friend whose communion had ever been pleasant – the most pleasant of all other friends, to whom you had ever turned with satisfaction . . .

If you had had a mother of our children who had cradled and nursed and trained them for the service of the living God, in which you most delighted; a mother indeed . . .

If you had had a wife, a sweet love of a wife, who for forty years had never given you real cause of grief; a wife who had stood with you side by side in the battle's front, who had been

44

a comrade to you, ever willing to interpose herself between you and the enemy and ever the strongest when the battle was fiercest . . .

My comrades, roll all these qualities into one personality and what would be lost in each I have lost, all in one . . . yet my heart is full of gratitude because God lent me for so long a season such a treasure.

I have never turned from her these forty years for any journeyings on my mission of mercy but I have longed to get back, and have counted the weeks, days, and hours which should take me again to her side. And now she has gone away for the last time. What, then, is there left for me to do? My work plainly is to fill up the weeks, the days, the hours, and cheer my poor heart as I go along with the thought that, when I have served my Christ and my generation according to the will of God – which I vow this afternoon I will, to the last drop of my blood – then I trust that she will bid me welcome to the skies, as He bade her.

*William Booth*

# On Being Single

If marriage is God's greatest gift to humankind, and that is how it may seem to those on the outside, for the grass is always greener on the other side of the fence, then why is it withheld or withdrawn from so many of his faithful followers, often women? It must remain one of the greatest mysteries of this life, offset only by the fact that Christ himself opted for the celibate life. What does become clear from the pain and the soul-searching of the women included here is that, no matter what society says, God means us to be whole people, whatever our status. And though the single woman may be forced to find her fulfilment outside that one special relationship, she will not have to do so alone. For she has a spiritual bridegroom, one who seems to make himself known and real to her in an almost physical way, certainly with an intimacy often denied her married sister.

*SUE BELL has very vivid dreams which she has always found a source of great inspiration and encouragement to her faith. This particular dream, which candidly reveals the vulnerability felt by many women who face life alone, came at a time when she had been particularly seeking fresh meaning and relevance to Easter.*

*She has been writing since she was a little girl and at present teaches drama in a Lancashire comprehensive school. She has just married at the age of 36.*

## The Dream

Parking lot
    car in sight
Woman, carrying shopping, makes her way past

two men
    waiting in parked car – watching
Feels menacing – feels alone
    Try not to panic.

Men, out of car – still watching
    Fumble for key – hand on shoulder
    Men are here

Horrid, leering face – promise of pain – fear
    God, where are you? You should be here
    You said you would – always.

Sudden start, thank God – only a dream.
But God, where were you? What does this mean?
Lying back on the pillow, I see:

    A man
In a garden – waiting
    Appointed time – coming soon.
Snaking its way up the hill an eerily lit procession.
    They're coming – it's time.

    Try not to panic
    Heart-beat – quicker
Suffocating fear, surrounding, blanket-like
    Can't breathe.
A traitor's kiss, faces of flint
    Surrounded by people – completely alone.
    'My God, my God, where are you?'

God, where are you in times like these?
Tell me, what does this mean?

My Son, waiting in the garden
    Surrounded by fear, cut off from me
      Completely alone
My child, in all your life, you will never be
    this alone.
My Son has seen to it – I will always
    be here
      for you.

*Sue Bell*

*The sense of 'aloneness' of the single person can be a heavy burden to bear. She misses that one special person who could be the recipient of all the loving she has to give. But such treasure need not be wasted. It can be converted into unexpected riches. As SUE ROSSETTER, a woman deacon from Pudsey, West Yorkshire, discovered one day, through an unexpected encounter.*

I remember a holiday in the South of England, when I strolled with a friend outside Salisbury Cathedral. My friend drew my attention to the tall, thin figure of a woman striding purposefully away from the magnificent building before us, her back towards the sublime certainties of its medieval architecture. The more I looked, the more she seemed to compel my gaze. I wanted to meet this stranger, to walk with her, talk with her . . . But this was foolish to the point of absurdity. For she was only a sculpture, a bronze statue of the Virgin Mary, immobilized on a solid plinth.

*Only* a sculpture? Yet she spoke to me that day in Salisbury Cathedral, through every mute line of her unyielding body.

I have a photograph of Elizabeth Frinks' 'Walking Madonna' before me as I write. There is little, I note with a measure of relief, to connect this straight-backed, angular woman with the blue and white madonnas of traditional art. Her face is austere. She is definitely middle-aged. And she is alone. Is *this* what draws me to her, I wonder? I too am forty-something, single, and sometimes hate both. There are times when the sense of loss borders on panic and threatens to overwhelm, as the certainties and endless possibilities of youth and marriage-ability dissolve in self-doubt and shrinking horizons. Oh, I know I'm not supposed to feel like this. Certain quarters of the media would have me believe that this is the era of the 'mature' woman who has cast off the limitations of youth and inexperience, and can at last compete with men on equal terms. The world, they say, is my oyster. Some, no doubt, find it so, but for me the oyster would appear to contain no pearl.

This 'Mary' would understand such feelings, I believe, for she has seen her pearl taken away from before her eyes, that pearl of great price, her firstborn son. And every line of her no longer youthful body speaks of the pain of that loss. But it speaks too of much gained, of a fruitfulness in which perhaps I share. For we have within ourselves, this Mary and I, a germ of knowledge, about ourselves, our fellows, our faith, that is the fruit of time, of experience and of a sometimes painful, sometimes lonely walk with God. And we *have* learned! From our sorrows, our losses and our gains. We have learned that there are truths, solid and substantial, that go deeper than easy platitudes and untested certainties.

Thank you, Lord, that in the middle years of my present singleness I walk with you and your blessed mother in an ever-increasing appreciation of the riches to be found and the gains to be won, through loss.

*Sue Rossetter*

50

## The Late Bride

And so she finally
after all those years
opened the box
And out flew
nothing
And was that all, she cried
there was in it?
Then why did I dream and yearn
scrabble and fight so long
to get my hands on it?

That was at first
it was only later she learnt
slowly, so slowly
to fill the box with
the treasures she had
unknowing, owned all along.

*Veronica Zundel*

*Part and parcel of coming to terms with singleness is the realization that marriage does not always live up to the glamorous fantasy woven by those who are denied it. But this can be a slow and painful process unless women, single and married, are prepared to share their dreams and admit their disappointments.*

*SUE HUNT, who teaches music and religious education in a Lancashire comprehensive school, was helped to that place of resolution when she finally understood how much one of her married friends envied her independence. Wholeness is not the prerogative of the woman with a partner. It is for both married and single alike to seek and discover.*

## Bride of Christ

Why are so few of us
satisfied with our lot?

There is a restlessness
        a dissatisfaction
        a discontent . . .

We long to be beautiful,
                wealthy
                interesting
                popular
                gifted
the list is endless –
single, we long for marriage
married, we long to be free.

We cling to the fantasies
which rob us of fulfilment
– fantasies woven by a society
        creating myths
        about marriage
which make the single person feel isolated
        and the married person pressurized.

Why do we torture ourselves, Lord?
Imagining –
Candlelit dinners for two,
orgasmic intimacy,
a lover
closer to us than our own breath,
Ignoring the whisper of common sense which says,
'It can't always be like that.'
And yet
we aren't entirely to blame.

Why, when I ask my doctor for a smear test
must I be forced to say that I am not sexually active?
And feel embarrassed,
ashamed?
Celibacy is not in vogue.
Yet You, who were a virgin all Your earthly life,
your sympathy
enfolds me
like a blanket.

A married friend of mine told me how
wistfully
she gazed in shoe shop windows
at smart court shoes
and matching handbag
symbolizing success,
      freedom,
        independence.

Whatever our status, we strive
after the mirages of fulfilment,
and as we come closer
they disappear
before our eyes.
How can we love, without first loving ourselves?
How can we marry, without first meeting ourselves?
We cripple others when we feed on them for fulfilment.

Lord, we are trapped on the merry-go-round of our striving,
holding on tight lest we fall off, as it whizzes round faster and
faster, leaving us increasingly breathless. The truth is that our
relationship with you, our spiritual husband, is barren; we
behave like spiritual whores, panting after other lovers, seeking
satisfaction in a multitude of other relationships, the cheap

rides. And you wait for us to face the pain of our spiritual poverty. You help us to get off the merry-go-round, wait for the dizziness to stop. Then, in the stillness, you come to us.

Woo us and win us, Lord, with the eagerness of a young bridegroom and the tenderness of a loving husband. Reassure us that we are altogether lovely in your eyes. Make us revel once more, in your healing touch, your unconditional love, which is the source of all our peace.

*Sue Hunt*

*To her neighbours in Amherst, Massachusetts, EMILY DICKIN-SON was an eccentric spinster, flitting around the house all dressed in white like a moth. From her twenties, possibly after a frustrated love for a married preacher, she became a recluse, only going out for occasional walks. The reality of her Christian faith is apparent in the two thousand or so poems discovered by her sister in a box after her death, some written on old envelopes and sweet papers. But she steadfastly refused to join a church.*

*This poem defiantly reminds those who dare pity the single woman that even she will have her wedding feast.*

### Eternity, I'm Coming

A wife at daybreak I shall be,
Sunrise, thou hast a flag for me?
At midnight I am yet a maid –
How short it takes to made it bride!
Then, Midnight, I have passed from thee
Unto the East and Victory.

Midnight, 'Good night'
I hear thee call.
The angels bustle in the hall,
Softly my Future climbs the stair,
I fumble at my childhood's prayer –
So soon to be a child no more!
Eternity, I'm coming, Sir –
Master, I've seen that face before.

*Emily Dickinson*

*CATHERINE MARSHALL (1913–90) was born in Canton, a small mid-Mississippi town, the daughter of a Presbyterian pastor. She married Peter Marshall, a Scotsman who made the United States his home and eventually became Chaplain to the Senate. Originally she had no other aim but to be 'the minister's wife', supporting her husband, promoting his career in any way she could. When he died quite suddenly only thirteen years after their marriage, leaving her with a nine-year-old son to bring up, she was forced to survive alone.*

I must realize that loneliness, that sense of dissatisfaction, that feeling of some happiness just eluding me, is in all human beings, and is put there by God to keep us searching after him. Perhaps when I just 'settle down' to this doubtful state of single blessedness, inner peace will come. We shall see.

Even five or six years after Peter's death I found that my journey through the valley was still a running battle with self-pity. Several of the couples on our street would often take a stroll in the early evening. Sometimes seeing them, I would think, *Were Peter still with me, he and I would be the youngest couple on this street. But no, our marriage is over.* Or at the theatre I would see a grey-haired man reach for his wife's hand, and I would wince with a passing pang of self-pity.

Or at a dinner party I would find myself the only single person there. Always I knew that my hostess had not meant to be thoughtless. It is hard for anyone who has known only an unbroken family to imagine how this particular situation makes the single person feel. Try as I might to overcome it, I would find that being in the presence of couples threw my aloneness into sharpest perspective.

What then is the solution? It must lie somewhere in the realm of relationship. As solitaries we can wither and die. We long to be needed; we yearn to be included; we thirst to know that we belong to someone. The question is – how can we achieve that sense of belonging?

There is a price to be paid. The first tribute exacted is a modicum of modesty with ourselves. On the one hand, do we want to be rid of loneliness so much that we will allow ourselves no more wallowing in the luxury of pity-parties? On the other hand, how badly do we want to make connection with other people? For let's admit it, there are pluses in having only oneself to think of.

In the light of honest answers to questions like these, I decided I need not be lonely unless I chose to be. The first step was recognizing the necessity for a new dimension and the decision to perform a freshening-up on myself. Having to make public appearances forced me to review my clothes situation. I found a specialist who, after studying my present wardrobe, my figure and my features, skilfully advised me on clothes shopping.

Then came some quiet reappraisal of certain restrictions my parents had placed upon me in my growing-up years. They had been so full of love for me that the taboos they had put on activities like ballroom dancing and bridge had mattered little to me – then.

But now as a widow in sophisticated Washington, I was embarrassed when someone asked me to dance. Or I had to decline an invitation to play bridge with friends.

The answer was to learn how – and I did. I enrolled for a series of lessons in ballroom dancing. Then three women friends and I set aside an evening a week to master bridge. We spread out teaching manuals on a second table beside us and learned the game together by playing it.

Seven years after Peter's death a change was taking place inside me without my being aware of it. While resigned to widowhood in my mind, emotionally I was preparing myself for a new kind of life.

*Catherine Marshall*


## For One-Parent Families

Father Almighty, help me in my special responsibility
of bringing up my children alone,
and look with love and understanding on all
one-parent families.

For the parents, help us to guide our children wisely,
and prevent us from conveying to them any bitterness,
resentment or self-pity that we may feel.

For the children, help them to establish close and lasting
relationships without fear of rejection or loss;
and in our homes grant us love, laughter and peace.

*Sylvia Jury*

# Pregnancy and Childbirth

Childbirth is a uniquely female experience. And though men are now permitted to share in it, to hold their partner's hand, mop the fevered brow, speak words of support and general encouragement, they can never fully enter into the ultimate act of human creativity. It was given to woman, admittedly with the promise of pain, though also with the promise of immense joy.

And it is this sense of wonder, awe and mystery which seems to prevail when women describe how it feels to be a 'bridge', the receptacle of new life. Of course, most of the thoughts and feelings recorded here have been set down after the event, have been analysed in retrospect. Perhaps if during the actual labour, paper and pencil were thrust into their hands, women might tell a very different story. My own pregnancies, involving long months of nausea and discomfort, were not the rosy-glowing, placidly-contented experiences I had been led to expect. And that was a shock. Jenny Cooke has described feeling similarly let down by the actual process of childbirth. Serena Lailey found breast-feeding a chore. But we all, nonetheless, gained from the experience, and not just because we held its precious produce in our hands. Being women and resilient, we managed to milk the experience for its spiritual truth.

In the early chapters of the Bible, when God warns woman that her struggle to make her body produce will parallel man's struggle to make the earth produce, he also tells her that she will commit herself wilfully to the process over and over again.

In an extraordinary reversal of Victorian, and even contemporary thinking, it is woman who will be overwhelmed by her desire for man. Bearing children is a living symbol of that special, God-given relationship.

But what then of the women who find that their desire for their man leads nowhere, women who are infertile? Are they any less woman? Women who have had difficult pregnancies or births, as Jenny Cooke did, have to come to terms with a sense of disappointment, the feeling that God has somehow let us down. Our faith is bolstered by the fact that unlike certain contemporary writings on the subject, the Scriptures never promised an easy, pain-free experience. It takes a far greater leap of faith to trust God when he appears to contradict himself altogether, and denies women the very thing for which their bodies were created.

*PENELOPE FLINT is a journalist. She wrote her autobiography* All the Days of My Life *when she was pregnant with her third child, cleverly interweaving her own growing spiritual development with the development of her unborn child, seeing in one a reflection of the other. In the seventh month of her pregnancy she was accepted as an oblate candidate by the Community of St Mary the Virgin in Wantage, an 'outside' member of the community, committed to the disciplines of prayer and meditation. It was the culmination of a long journey of inner searching begun when she was a student in Oxford.*

I wanted to be a bridge and I am one.
Stretched over the abyss
between two worlds,
that of the not yet being –

abstract, intangible, always present –
and that of the manifest –
crude, hard, singular world of mass and shape,
motion and noise, separate being.

My body is the bridge for I am a woman.
It is the door between the worlds.

Wrapped in serenity, inmost concentration,
the new comes into being
through my door
which quivers and groans
almost rocked back into the first world
by the shock.

And still, afterwards, when the new thing
safely arrived, suckles,
my body is still the bridge
having to reconcile impossible contraries –
inner and outer, subject and object,
formless and formed, first and second,
the two worlds.

*Penelope Flint*

*LUCY GUINNESS KUMM (1865–1906), with her husband Karl, founded the Sudan United Mission at the turn of the century. Her anthology of poems entitled* Motherhood, *'by one who fathomed its pain, as well as its bliss', deemed 'too sacred' for publication in her lifetime, was published anonymously more than twenty years after her death. Even then it was an enormous sales success for Longmans the publishers. No one had dared to write so intimately before on so delicate a subject as pregnancy.*

*Sadly, the prayer in one of her poems that she should die before her child, a realistic rather than a morbid pre-occupation in Victorian times, was answered sooner than she might have wished. She died of an untreated ectopic third pregnancy when her two boys were very young. Her elder sister, who had had two miscarriages and was subsequently unable to have any children, brought them up as her own.*

Why should she welcome months of fear and strain,
   Grey sleepless nights and burdened, weary days,
   Hampered exertion and constricted ways,
Lost youth and beauty, ne'er to come again?
Why, were there nothing priceless to attain,
   Should she with calmness undertake to face
   Anguish no tongue can tell, nor memory trace,
Death threatening silent, just beyond the pain?

Why, when th'essential suffering is o'er
   Should she forego for days and nights of loss
   (Service which many would account a cross)
Free, lightsome hours, the springtide life of yore?
   Ask, and in answer she hath simply smiled:
   Lo, to her heart she clasps a little child.

*Lucy Guinness Kumm*

*JENNY COOKE was one of the first Christian writers to write about childbirth. It was not, she said, that completely natural, deeply satisfying, extraordinarily wonderful experience it was purported to be. In fact, after an extremely difficult first birth she felt let down, by the 'natural childbirth' techniques, and by God, whom she presumed would make it easy for her. It took her a year to come to terms with the experience, and even longer to form a happy, relaxed relationship with her new son.*

*Recording her feelings was part of the healing process. And in so doing she brought comfort to many women who had suffered extreme distress during childbirth, felt inadequate and a failure afterwards, and had not found the bonding process with their new baby as easy as they had been led to expect.*

## The Firstborn

There was no joy when you were born
Dear son, for pain so bit and cracked me
That tears were a release
Denied.
Nurses, to ease themselves,
Fibbed with drugs, while you
Reluctant, would not come.
It took blunt, cold blades to wrench you out.

A flaxen baby, plaited cord stretched
Green from shrunken womb hung limp
As dead.
At last your instinct groped a cry.
They placed you in obedient arms:
Too weak to welcome
My heart a vacuum.

63

Agony gone,
I passed through sterile corridors
To sleep's illusion.
Then joy dawned at my shocked core:
Firstborn son,
The desire of kings,
You are mine.

*Jenny Cooke*

*One of America's foremost religious poets, LUCI SHAW(b.1928)
nonetheless grew up in England, Australia and Canada. She
married an American, Harold Shaw, and they ran a publishing
company together. Since his death she has divided her time
between Illinois, where they used to live together, and the
West Coast, where she runs poetry and creativity workshops.
She has published five collections of poems and a book on
her bereavement.*

    *With five children of her own, now all grown up, childbirth
is hardly unfamiliar to her. Here she uses her own experience
to explore the great mystery of God reduced to a foetus,
subject to the limitations of a woman's body. But this particular
pregnancy and birth enshrines the key to eternal life, for every
woman, and every man.*

## Made Flesh

After
the bright beam of hot annunciation
fused heaven with dark earth
his searing sharply-focused light
went out for a while

64

eclipsed in amniotic gloom:
his cool immensity of splendour
his universal grace
small-folded in a warm dim
female space –
the Word stern-sentenced
to be nine months dumb –
infinity walled in a womb
until the next enormity –
the Mighty, after submission
to a woman's pains
helpless on a barn-bare floor
first-tasting bitter earth.

Now
I in him surrender
to the crush and cry of birth.
Because eternity
was closeted in time
he is my open door
to forever.
From his imprisonment my freedoms grow,
find wings.
Part of his body, I transcend this flesh.
From his sweet silence my mouth sings.
Out of his dark I glow.
My life, as his,
slips through death's mesh,
time's bars,
joins hands with heaven,
speaks with stars.

*Luci Shaw*

## The Grandchild

As a young mother, looking with disbelief, incredulity and shock upon the still-born face of my first daughter, I would have said a baby was misery and mystery.

Later on, lying in hospital, with my second, perfect girl in my arms, not quite choirs of angels, but nurses in capes carolling by lantern-light around our bed, a baby was joy, triumph, fulfilment. I was not to know then that it also meant years of lasting love.

Learning that the three-pound scrap of life in the incubator was my third, invalid, daughter, meant a baby was a disaster. The six months of her life were a rage of grief, betrayal, rebellion and pure pain. Her death was part relief, part regret, wholly devastating.

I never saw a baby with my heart after that, so the first sight of my new-born grandson caught me unawares. My first impulse was to kneel. I would have said then that a baby was a small touch from the hand of God.

Now, with another happy, laughing grandson to love, a baby is – what? Hope, perhaps, or promises? Or reassurances that there is some reason in the scheme of things.

What is a baby? It is Life, of course. What else?

*Frances Mary Marston*


As long as there are babies in the world the age of miracles will never cease.

All mothers know this.

To look at that dainty, breathing, moving creature lying in its curtained cot with its own energy and volition, its own world and life, its private joys and sorrows, pains and satisfaction – to look at it and think that a few months ago it had no existence and that to you and another its presence on earth is due, is to realize yourself in the presence of a miracle compared with which all but one other pale.

For this to which you have given birth is a life which will *go on*. How far? How long? And whither? Bearing what in its train? And with what consequences?

Before such questions who can stand?

But there is a further question even more overwhelming, a question every parent must face. 'What in my past impels my child either to rise or fall?'

Have you ever met that question, put not by your own spirit, not by any written or spoken word of God or man, but coming to you directly, clear as the cry of your baby, solemn as a voice from the dead, from the innocent eyes of your new-born child?

*Lucy Guinness Kumm*

She is yours to hold in your cupped hands, to guard and to guide. Give her your strength and wisdom and all the good that life can offer. Yours is a sacred trust. Never harm her with words that can bite and sting. Lead her into truth.

These words were written down for us when our miracle baby daughter was born. Our firstborn had been made to order. He was planned, with maximum convenience to his parents, around our summer holiday abroad. And I therefore presumed that I held the key to life in my own hands. A dangerous thing, presumption!

No second child appeared. We had not, after all, the power to will a new life into existence. Certain 'women's problems', as male doctors love to call them, were preventing conception. Months of gynaecological probing and prodding ensued. Why God has hidden those crucial female organs away is a mystery to me. I was alternately deep frozen and roasted, like a piece of raw meat, to no avail.

Neighbours, gentle, reliable, heaven-sent neighbours prayed for me when I landed on their doorstep one day in tears, utterly disheartened by the news that further surgery was needed before there would be any baby.

'Come back in two weeks', my G.P. had said, prescribing an intensive course of antibiotics, 'and I'll refer you, again, to a consultant.'

I went back in two weeks – with a sample in a little glass bottle – for a pregnancy test. Our beloved little bundle of giggles and joy was on the way. Fortunately her journey into being was hidden from me then!

No bouncing, blooming serenity mine. No expansive, bovine, placid months of waiting. Nine months of incessant vomiting, shivering and discomfort. Scarlet fever rocketed my temperature and covered my expanding body in oozing pores and bleeding sores. She sat in the womb, pushing her head up into my stomach and diaphragm. I couldn't digest, couldn't breathe, could think no positive, soothing thoughts to encourage her on her way to this world.

And then she arrived – not in the mother-controlled, gentle, meditative way I had planned, the way the natural childbirth pundits promised – but in a numbing, mind-spinning panic. They turned her in the womb. Her heart all but stopped. They induced her, breaking the waters. And down came the cord. It slithered in the doctor's hands, and I saw the panic in his eyes. How many minutes between this second and brain damage? Between brain damage and death? I couldn't remember.

But felt no panic, only wave upon wave of peace, as I knelt on the trolley, head well down, to keep that baby off the cord, as they wheeled me down the corridors to the operating theatre. 'Her name will be faithful. Her hand will never leave his, and his hand will never cease to protect her all her life long.'

The words, given to me for her months before, when we had prayed for the protection of the foetus from the effects of scarlet fever, floated into my mind as I drifted into unconsciousness.

And then, there she was, curled up in a cot next to me, an easy, contented, restful baby, who would grow into a relaxed, merry little girl, belying the trauma of her journey here. But oh how vulnerable. How I have prayed that no biting, stinging word of mine, no inadvertent word of bitterness or sarcasm, jealousy or malice, would poison or diminish the joyous, loving, laughing gift I have held in my cupped hands for the last eleven years. An awesome responsibility for a mother, to lead a daughter into truth.

*Michele Guinness*

*SERENA LAILEY's baby, Kezi, was quite a 'late arrival', and though having a baby when you're older than the average parents may not be easy, it does bring its own special pleasure. Serena gave up her job as a teacher when Kezi was born, to give her, if not the best of her energy, the benefit of her experience and maturity!*

## Breastfeeding

Breastfeeding my tiny daughter Keziah was something of an endurance test for me and throughout those five long months there was much discomfort and gritting of teeth, not to mention curling of toes! However, as so often happens, God taught me an interesting spiritual lesson from this natural, physical process. As I sat for many hours in the little den I had made myself in my bedroom, the baby propped up on a large pillow on my lap, I pondered that breastfeeding was yet another example of the way in which his design of our physical world mirrors some of the great principles of the outworkings of his love in our spiritual world.

69

All the books had told me not to give up if my milk supply seemed inadequate and not to reach for a bottle of man-made powdered milk but instead to give the baby more feeds. This giving would increase my supply: miraculously my body would simply respond to the demanding sucks of my baby and produce more milk. I would need no more food or drink in order to achieve this, just simply devote more time to feeding my baby. This led me to reflect that in so many situations we cry out to God, 'I can't cope', forgetting his endless resources are there. We just need to devote more time to him so that he can replenish us. Perhaps Luke 6.38 could form part of a chapter heading in a breastfeeding manual: 'Give to others and God will give to you. Indeed you will receive a full measure, a generous helping . . .' Irreverent? I hope not for I believe that God's design cannot fail to be perfect.

*Serena Lailey*

*FIONA DUNCAN is a social worker living in Coventry. Her pain at being unable to have a child was like a long bereavement, exacerbated by the fact that her job involved taking children 'at risk' into care. Her story is a vivid example of a faith which begs for attention and recognition, even when mystery threatens to overwhelm it.*

I remember so well the feelings of anticipation that we shared as we walked along a railway embankment one lazy summer day in 1987, the day we decided to start a family. We had put it off for the two years since our marriage, wanting to be fully prepared for what we viewed as one of the most important phases of our life.

Naïvely we thought we were having our last summer holiday alone together, that I would be pregnant upon our return. It did not happen and, as the months passed, puzzlement gave way to disappointment, as we realized that parenthood was not something within our control.

A visit to our GP in June 1988 started us along a road of despair, devastation, confusion and pain we never dreamed could exist. In December we were told that we had only 1 per cent chance of ever conceiving a child. And the bottom fell out of our world. Why had God done this to us? What had we done to deserve it?

My sexuality was challenged profoundly. Women were made to bear children. If I could not experience this was I a real woman? I found myself feeling the need to be attractive to other men, to prove to myself that I was a woman.

Though I loved him dearly, I even wanted my husband to be free to divorce me, although his was the fertility problem. I wanted him to have the opportunity to find someone who did not want a child, who would not make him feel he had let her down. Thank God he loved me enough to cope with my pain and anger, as well as his own.

Our families were waiting for a grandchild, niece, nephew, cousin, and I could not provide what was expected of me. 'Just relax and it will happen', friends said to me, not meaning to patronize, 'At least you can adopt', they said. But my arms ached for my own child, my whole body longed to feel the kick of my developing child.

Throughout these months we continued with the investigations and treatments. We were suddenly forced into having to consider the ethical implications of what we were doing. We often felt we were walking a moral and ethical tightrope, trying to decide not only what was acceptable to us, but to God.

The physical impact of the treatment was in itself a trauma we had not counted on. The constant examinations, injections and scans were the most harrowing. The drugs had considerable side-effects: hot flushes, nausea and mood swings. We were on a see-saw of emotions. Hope in another new treatment, the optimism of the doctors, sent us skyward. Another period, each like a miscarriage with no baby to grieve for, plunged me down into the depths.

I came to a point when I knew I could not go on. I was utterly spent, emotionally and spiritually. I needed help and found a counsellor, not a Christian counsellor for I was afraid of being judged 'a bad Christian'.

The sessions that followed were painful and difficult. They took me on a voyage of self-discovery, and I was reluctant to continue for fear of what I might find out about myself. In fact, I discovered a gentle, sensitive, caring person, who did not need to be a wife, mother or career woman to be of value to God, or the world.

The pain of childlessness did not go away. The yearning to be a mother did not fade. But there was a growing awareness that my pain did not make me unlovable. It simply made me more vulnerable, more sensitive to other people's crises, more able to love others unconditionally, as God loved me.

We are one of the fortunate couples. I am now the proud mother of twins after a second attempt at *in vitro* fertilization. We could of course claim a miracle. But then every child is a miracle. The four years of crisis have not been wasted, or negated, because I have a child at last. My relationship with God has changed. He is no longer distant, for I have shouted at him, fought him, fled from him, grappled with him, been ruthlessly honest with him; and it hasn't driven him away. I still have many unanswered questions about why our pregnancy had to be so medicalized, so unspontaneous. But there is rest at last.

*Fiona Duncan*

# On Being Mum

With the birth over, the baby safe in arms, the whole complex process of mothering is about to begin. Being a mother can be a source of immense joy, inspire feelings of enormous tenderness and responsibility, or it can cause great pain. It can be all three at different times in a woman's experience. When it works well it can prove to be one of the most powerful images of God's love for human beings. When it doesn't work it leaves a bucketful of guilt and anguish behind in the children who have been denied their instinctive rights to protection and love.

'What in my past impels my child to rise or fall?' asked Lucy Guinness Kumm in the last section. The question seems to hover over many of the experiences recorded here, for mothering can bring out the best and the worst in us – which is why it is such a powerful source of guilt for so many women. We can never live up to the idealized standards set by society, let alone our own.

In his extraordinary book, *The Prophet*, Kahlil Gibran summarized the tension of bringing up children when he said:

> You may give them your love, but not your thoughts,
> For they have their own thoughts.
> You may house their bodies but not their souls,
> For their souls dwell in the house of tomorrow, which you
> cannot visit, not even in your dreams.

Our duty is to point our children, like arrows from the bow, in the right direction. Where the arrow lands is beyond our control. But let them go, we must, for 'The first important matter for a parent to settle in her own mind is this: to whom does this child belong? Is it mine, or is it the Lord's?' says Catherine Booth, mother of the Salvation Army. That letting go, that severing of the umbilical cord, can seem like a surgical operation, leaving us drained and empty, forced to rediscover who we are again, as separate entities from those who are so much a part of ourselves.

Dear God and Mother of all Humanity
whose tenderness is reflected in the beauty of a mother
suckling her child,
help me to witness to the worth of personal values and the
need of gentleness and compassion in a mass-produced and
impersonal world.

*Phoebe Willetts*

*MOTHER TERESA is without doubt one of the giants of the faith. She was born into a close, loving Albanian peasant home. She found it hard to leave her family and homeland, to take up the calling she received when she was still a child, to go to the poorest of the poor. But she chose to obey the call, to give herself to Christ and to her neighbour, and in so doing, like so many others before her, found a life fuller and richer than she ever dared to imagine. One woman's obedience led to the founding of an order which now has houses in India, Australia, Latin America, Italy and all over the world.*

Today there is so much trouble in the world and I think that much of it begins at home. The world is suffering so much because there is no peace. There is no peace because there is no peace in the family and we have so many thousands and thousands of broken homes. We must make our homes centres of compassion and forgive endlessly and so bring peace.

Make your house, your family, another Nazareth where love, peace, joy and unity reign, for love begins at home. You must start there and make your home the centre of burning love. You must be the hope of eternal happiness to your wife, your husband, your child, to your grandfather, grandmother, to whoever is connected with you.

Do you know the poor of your own home first? Maybe in your home there is somebody who is feeling very lonely, very unwanted, very handicapped. Maybe your husband, your wife, your child is lonely. Do you know that?

The home is where the mother is. Once I picked up a child and took him to our children's home, gave him a bath, clean clothes, everything, but after a day the child ran away. Then I said to the Sisters, 'Please follow that child. One of you stay with him and see where he goes when he runs away.' And the child ran away a third time. There under a tree was the mother. She had put two stones under an earthenware vessel and was cooking something she had picked up from the dustbins. The Sister asked the child, 'Why did you run away from the home?' And the child said: 'But this is my home, because this is where my mother is.'

Mother was there. That was home. That the food was taken from the dustbins was all right because mother had cooked it. It was mother that hugged the child, mother who wanted the child and the child had its mother. Between a wife and a husband it is the same . . . Smile at one another. It is not always easy. We must give Jesus a home in our homes for only then can we give him to others.

*Mother Teresa*

*Those of us who are mothers may be tempted to say, 'It's all right for Mother Teresa. She has never known the sheer fatigue involved in bringing up children, the endless demands we face, minute by minute, which so easily wipe the smile off our faces and rob us of any opportunity for tranquillity of spirit and prayerfulness.'*

*ANGELA ASHWIN, who spent seven years in Swaziland, helping to train future clergy, has three children, all teenagers now. She leads retreats, quiet days and courses on spirituality, which all aim to interweave prayer with the ordinary ingredients of everyday. She captures so well here the frustrations of a mother who still wants to guard some space for God and for herself. She may be forced to abandon more traditional forms of spirituality, which involve finding five minutes quiet (a forgotten luxury when your child even follows you to the toilet), to find a new, more relevant kind of spirituality altogether.*

. . . Just back from holiday – piles of letters to answer and papers to read – trying to finish unpacking – 'Mummy, can we do some painting?' – 'Please would you mend the chain on my bike?' – 'Where's my hairbrush?' – 'Mummy, my knitting's in a knot' . . .

. . . Just changing the baby when a voice from downstairs calls, 'I've just fallen over in the nettles' – searching frantically for the soothing cream when the doorbell goes . . .

. . . It's nearly tea time and we haven't enough bread – we must put on wellies to go to the shop because it is raining hard – while hunting the telephone rings – during that phone call the toddler has gone into the muddy back garden in his socks . . .

This harassed mother has to find what might be called a vertical wholeness in the middle of the 'horizontal' incompleteness around her. Wholeness, for her, is to be found in the way she looks at her children's paintings, answers their questions and picks them up when they fall over. Wholeness lies in trying to love and remain Christ-centred in the present moment; and the present moment is very often an interruption.

*Angela Ashwin*

*After fourteen years as a nun, CLARE RICHARDS left the convent. Later she married Bert, an ex-priest. Their struggle to have a family took them all the way to South America where, in 1980, after many set-backs, they finally succeeded in adopting twin babies born in a remote village in the Andes. As the mother of Pedro and Blanca, Clare realized how sheltered she had been from the reality of the daily grind, especially for mothers. She began to understand her life and faith in quite a new way. Recently she has returned to part-time teaching and writing books for schools.*

I remember having a very romantic idea of Mary. She is, of course, the ideal woman, the virgin, held up as the model for nuns. Her motherhood is dehumanized first by insisting on the importance of her 'virginity' and second by transferring her mothering of Jesus to her mothering of 'the Church'. For mothers themselves Mary is also held up as a model. But the effectiveness of her example is ruined by the doctrines which surround her. I remember the occasion which forced me to analyse the position of Mary in our Catholic thinking.

Pedro, aged five and ever cheerful, was humming and singing all day. He was going through his school repertoire and, like a record stuck in a groove, he was repeating over and over again the line, 'The little Lord Jesus, no crying he makes'. In between the singing we had tears and quarrels. Bianca was fed up with Pedro's cheerfulness. She mucked up his game of cars. I got cross. More tears. As the day wore on the idea of a perfect, non-crying baby Jesus and a composed mother Mary really annoyed me. What a mother needs to know is that all children are the same and that other mums lose patience. As a Catholic mother exhorted to look to Mary as a model for motherhood, I want her, in fact I need her to have experienced the same tiredness and frustrations. It makes no sense that Jesus didn't cry as a baby. If he didn't, he wasn't human.

Is he supposed never to have thrown a two-year-old tantrum? Never to have stamped a three-year-old's foot and shouted 'No'? Never to have whined and wanted his own way *now* as a four-year-old? If Mary was spared our common mother experiences of the more painful kind, I don't think she can be our example. When I walk around a supermarket and see a mother dragging an unwilling youngster round or losing patience with an insistent 'wanting, wanting' child, I feel very close to that mum. I know exactly how tired she feels. I now presume that Mary is close to us in this same way and joins in the sense of community that I feel with all mothers. She has been there too.

*Clare Richards*


*Each child is a gift, even if the packaging comes as quite a shock. And each experience of mothering can be a revelation. For some women the experience of mothering is especially bitter-sweet, requiring super-human measures of tenderness and patience to overcome the initial disappointment.*

*Teacher and writer CAROLINE PHILPS had no warning that*

78

*her first child would not be the 'perfect' baby she expected. But despite the shock she discovered inner reserves she never knew existed until Lizzie came into her life. Lizzie brought her own very special love, and showed Caroline that a mother can teach even the bird with clipped wings to fly.*

Saturday 11th April, 1981

I cried a lot last night. A nurse brought me in some tea and said, 'You'll be all right. You've got faith, haven't you?' Why are my personal beliefs suddenly everyone else's property? How does she know it will be so easy? . . .

Was it only last night the paediatrician asked to see my husband? The nurse told me when I first went to see my new baby daughter at 5 p.m. I thought there must be something wrong and I looked down at the tiny person in my arms; an expression, or was it the shape of her face, reminded me of something. And then I knew. 'She's a mongol, isn't she?' I said to the nurse. 'They don't know yet', she replied. But I knew. I bravely said that I was a Christian and God must have a good purpose in giving her to us. The nurse praised my attitude. But I said to my daughter, 'You'll be the brainiest mongol out', and tried hard not to cry.

Mark came as soon as I'd managed to telephone him – I hated telling him over the phone – I felt guilty. He'd just been telling our family and friends that we had a daughter. Now he would have to phone again. I felt I'd failed him. I hadn't managed to have a normal baby, like the other mothers in the hospital. I was relieved to discover that Mark had spent half an hour with her when I was being stitched up. He hadn't noticed anything wrong then and just thought she was a very sweet little baby. I sensed that he loved her despite everything. But I tried to be brave for him . . .

When I awoke this morning, very early, I thought for a

second that it was all a terrible dream. Then the sickening thud at the pit of my stomach told me otherwise. I spent the day in utter desperation longing to see my daughter. I asked several nurses when I could go down and couldn't believe it when they said I'd have to wait until after their tea-break. When eventually I was escorted towards the special baby-care unit the excitement and tension mounted.

I'd only held her for half an hour in the first twenty-four hours of her life. Would I love her? Would the gap of time when I hadn't seen her put a barrier between us? Could I accept her? Why did I have to fight the feeling of revulsion and alienation when I thought that her body wasn't made in quite the same way as ours?

I pushed open the swing doors. And there she was – such a tiny creature. I hated the stockinette cap and mittens taped over her hands, the aertex nightie that swamped her. It made her more alien. I wanted to cuddle her, and the hat kept falling off into her eyes. She was wrapped up tightly in a sheet and given to me to hold. I sat in a chair in a room full of incubators and held her close and talked to her.


Sunday 12th April

I was allowed to move down into the special baby-care unit today. I couldn't believe that I could have my daughter with me all the time. I just lay on the bed and listened to her breathing . . . it was so amazing to think that she belonged to me. She had such tiny hands and face.

I read my Bible for the first time since she was born. Psalms 61 and 62 were the reading for the day, and one verse jumped out at me from the page: 'You have heard my promises, O God, and you have given me what belongs to those who honour you.'

That was how I was meant to understand our little daughter, as a gift, a special gift. We had thought we would call a daughter Sarah, but somehow it didn't fit. I felt that we should call her Elizabeth, Elizabeth Joy. Elizabeth because it means 'gift or promise of God' and Joy because I knew we should be confident that she would bring us much joy. It was an act of faith at this moment but we could be sure God would honour that faith in him and in our daughter.

*Caroline Philps*

*JANE GRAYSHON's children are adopted. Years of intense pain following an operation resulted in a hysterectomy when she was still in her early thirties. Forced to help other women to give birth, it was a heavy cross for a midwife to bear. For Jane, still living with the possibility of illness and death, mothering is a particularly precious gift. She has learned to treasure each moment and to see in it a parable of how God loves his children.*

## To My Son
*and my heavenly Father*

The times I most treasure
were those feeds in the night
I used to creep through
at first sound of your cry

And you lay in my arms
and you gazed as you looked
and I rocked in the chair
and I sang
and you cooed

81

We'd have melted the frosts
by the warmth in our hearts
When the works was asleep
and they danced in their dreams
We danced in our eyes

And that is the closeness
You long for, my Father.
Yet I'm blind to your tenderness
and shrink from your hold
Rouse me from slumber
to lie in your arms
And gaze in sheer wonder
at the warmth in your eyes.

*Jane Grayshon*

## The Love that Passes Knowledge

Can it be possible that God loves human souls as much as I love my child – with this unutterable tenderness; with this longing pity, sympathy, comprehension; with this passion of desire to protect, supply, sustain? What would I not give my baby? Life's all, unhesitatingly! What would I not do, if I but could? And He can.

And He says: 'Yes, they may forget,' even mothers, 'yet will not I forget thee.'

*Lucy Guinness Kumm*

*MOTHER JULIAN OF NORWICH (1342–1416) experienced her sixteen extraordinary revelations, or 'showings' as she calls them, on 8th May 1373 when she was recovering from an illness. It appears she was still living at her mother's house at the time and only became a recluse later, some time before 1400. Her fame as a spiritual counsellor spread way beyond Norwich, and though her writings have inspired and delighted thousands down through the centuries, she claimed she was 'a simple creature, unlettered'. For Julian God was 'Mother' rather than Father.*

## Our True Mother, Jesus

A mother's is the most intimate, willing and dependable of all services, because it is the truest of all. None has been able to fulfil it properly but Christ, and he alone can. We know that our own mother's bearing of us was a bearing to pain and death, but what does Jesus, our true mother, do?

Why, he, All-love, bears us to joy and to eternal life! Blessings on him! And he is in labour until the time has fully come for him to suffer the sharpest pangs and most appalling pain possible – and in the end he dies. And not when this is over, and we ourselves have been born to eternal bliss, is his marvellous love completely satisfied.

He might die no more, but that does not stop him working, for he needs to feed us . . . it is an obligation of his dear, motherly love. A mother will suckle her child with her own milk, but our beloved mother Jesus feeds us with himself, and, with most tender courtesy, does it by means of the Blessed Sacrament, the precious food of all true life. The human mother may put her child tenderly to her breast, but our tender Mother Jesus simply leads us into his blessed breast through his open side, and there gives us a glimpse of the Godhead and heavenly joy – the inner certainty of eternal bliss.

In essence motherhood means love and kindness, wisdom, knowledge, goodness. Though in comparison with our spiritual birth our physical birth is a small, unimportant, straightforward sort of thing, it still remains that it is only through his working that it can be done at all by his creatures.

*Julian of Norwich*

*Once the children are old enough to take their first, tentative steps out of the nest, the years of real anxiety and anguish begin. For as soon as the fledglings realize what fun independence is, they begin to tug harder and harder on the umbilical cord. 'Where is she?' 'Did you say he could stay out this late?' 'Ought we to call the police?' There is a sense in which we learn to pray as never before, and are forced to trust and let go.*

*JENNY ROBERTSON (b.1942) was a social worker, until caring for her children and an elderly mother kept her at home and she returned to her first love of writing. She has written several novels for children, two collections of poems and a play. All her work is inspired by her faith, her concern for justice and for the status of women. She and her husband travel regularly to Eastern Europe to support Christians there.*

### Three a.m. – A Mother Waits

Nuns keep vigil with psalm and measured voice;
nurses manoeuvre amidst moans and snores.
Rocked against the long-drawn ticking night,
dry-mouthed, driven from sleep, I wait,
imagine in each bang and in each engine noise
the overdue return, the rasping key.

84

Get up, grope for his empty bed and pray
no less devoutly than devoted soeurs,
as anxiously as nurses watch for day.
Morning is now four short hours away.
The wind blows litter over silent streets.
Dossers and drunks find huddled brief respite
and junkies dream gaunt nightmares. My fears
fuse with relief and fury – the boy appears.

*Jenny Robertson*

*Celtic spirituality has a life all of its own. It grew out of the
songs and hymns, tales and stories, the unique way of life and
cultural tradition of the people who lived on the barren, rocky
desolate Hebridean islands off the coast of Scotland. The
Celtic scholar, Alexander Carmichael, spent a lifetime collecting
these prayers and poems together, incorporating them in the
six-volume* Carmina Gaedelica.

*In the Celtic tradition prayer and work are fully integrated,
and a mother would have chanted this prayer for her absent
child continually as she went about her daily business, milking
the cows or tending the household.*

### The Mother's Blessing
*(A Celtic Prayer)*

Where thou shalt bring the crown of thy head,
    Where thou shalt bring the tablet of thy brow,
Strength be to thee therein,
    Blest be to thee the powers therein;
    Strength be to thee therein;
    Blest be to thee the powers therein.

85

Lasting be thou in thy lying down,
    Lasting be thou in thy rising up,
Lasting be thou by night and day,
    And surpassing good be heaven to my dear one;
    Lasting be thou by day and by day,
    And surpassing good be heaven to my dear one.

The face of God be to thy countenance,
The face of Christ the kindly,
The face of the Spirit Holy
    Be saving thee each hour
    In danger and in sorrow:
        Be saving thee each hour
        In danger and in sorrow.


## Parting From My Son

The plane wheels lurch, leave
the tarmac, tightening
the inescapable cord.
The tug
brings sudden tears. No use to call myself
a fool. Time has no help for
what ails me.

Son, grown to a colossus, striding
the streets in your high boots, spinning
your gaudy fantasies,
your desperado moustache is
no disguise to me.

I leave you where the wind
blows cold off the river

your dreams are not enough
to keep me warm.

*Evangeline Paterson*

I had the privilege of hearing the late Frank Lake, founder of Clinical Theology, preach his last sermon. And one anecdote in particular has stayed with me ever since. Like a jackdaw pecking on a tree trunk, it has failed to leave me at peace with rigid, diehard attitudes when I have been tempted to dismiss certain individuals as being awkward just for the sake of it.

He described how one day a mother, a professional woman, came to ask his advice about one of her children. The other three, she said, were helpful, considerate, malleable and Christian. But this daughter was awkward, unhelpful, aggressive, and anti-religion. Would he see her?

He agreed, but on one condition: he must interview the whole family, separately and together. She consented. And he went on to say that it became abundantly clear, from the beginning of the interview, that the 'difficult' daughter was the only truly sane, truly honest member of the family.

'Always', he said, 'look out for and listen to the square peg in the round hole. Because in these days of plastic relationships, plastic families, and even plastic churches, who knows whether the thorn in the flesh is not the lone voice of integrity and truth?'

*Michele Guinness*

# Daddy's Girl

---

'But my heart belongs to Daddy.' So says the old, familiar song, and many a girl knows how true that is. Equally, just as the relationship with mother can be fraught with pain and tension, the very idea of father may have extremely negative associations, colouring a woman's relationship with the God Christians call 'Our Father'. This is particularly so when there has been some form of abuse in childhood. Rejection by the male parent leaves a woman with a difficult journey towards self-acceptance. But whether 'Daddy' is Phyllis McGinley's dragon-seeking hero, or the ogre who acknowledged our existence only with a curse, he carves himself a great hole out of our lives and we feel empty when he has gone.

*PHYLLIS McGINLEY (1905–78) was born in Oregon to a Roman Catholic family. She graduated from the University of Utah, worked as an English teacher, an advertising copywriter and a poetry editor. She won the Pulitzer Prize for poetry in 1960. The 'lightness' of her verse forms can often mask her profound insights into the ironies of life, particularly the foibles of men.*

### First Lesson

A thing to remember about fathers is, they're men.
A girl has to keep it in mind.

89

They are dragon-seekers, bent on improbable rescues.
Scratch any father, you'll find
Someone chock-full of qualms and romantic terrors,
Believing change is a threat –
Like your first shoes with heels on, like your first bicycle
It took such months to get.

Walk in strange woods, they warn you about the snakes
    there.
Climb, and they fear you'll fall.
Books, angular boys, or swimming in deep water –
Fathers mistrust them all.
Men are worriers. It is difficult for them
To learn what they must learn:
How you have a journey to take and very likely,
For a while, will not return.

*Phyllis McGinley*

*ELAINE FEINSTEIN is a prolific writer, with several novels and books of poetry to her credit. Born in Lancashire, but raised in Leicestershire, hers was a secure, happy childhood. Though she went on to read English at Newnham College, Cambridge, she admired the father who had left school at twelve, had no time for books, and only believed in luck and hard work in the running of his small business. He was an optimist and a dreamer and she loved him for it, that and his 'gentleness, physical strength and indomitable courage'.*

*Her sense of security was shattered when, after the war, she discovered what had happened to many Jewish children like her in Hitler's camps. Though she had been raised in the security of an assimilated British family, it was a long time before she felt able to trust anyone again.*

## Dad

Your old hat hurts me, and those black
fat raisins you liked to press into
my palm from your soft heavy hand:
I see you staggering back up the path
with sacks of potatoes from some local farm,
fresh eggs and flowers. Every day I grieve

for your great heart broken and you gone.
You loved to watch the trees. This year
you did not see their Spring.
The sky was freezing over the fen
as on that somewhere secretly appointed day
you beached: cold, white-faced, shivering.

What happened, old bull, my loyal
hoarse-voiced warrior? The hammer
blow that stopped you in your track
and brought you to a hospital monitor
could not destroy your courage
to the end you were
uncowed and unconcerned with pleasing anyone.

I think of you now as once again safely
at my mother's side, the earth as
chosen as a bed, and feel most sorrow for
all that was gentle in
my childhood buried there
already forfeit, now forever lost.

*Elaine Feinstein*

*Poets Elaine Feinstein and Phyllis McGinley had great affection for fathers who loved and protected them. But many women of their generation are not so fortunate. Fathering does not always come naturally or easily to men, particularly if social norms discourage them from demonstrating any tenderness.*

*But ANN NEEDHAM, who manages the Granary coffee bar at St Thomas' Church in Lancaster discovered that, however unlikely the possibility, it is never too late to discover that special relationship.*

He never seemed to notice me.
And when he did, it was to scorn and hurt.
'You can't have a lift. The others can. You can walk.'
Why? What had I done?
The last of five children, was I an afterthought, an
    unwelcome surprise, another
mouth to feed, body to clothe, that he pretended I wasn't
    there,
counted for nothing?
I never knew.
But grew,
from child to woman
with no male touch or scent,
encouragement, pride or approval.

Until the very end,
when He who had become a real Father to me, became a
    Father to him,
and taught him to father.
He held out a hand to me,
an upturned palm hanging in mid-air,
stretched across a lifetime of denial and neglect,
begging forgiveness, acceptance, reconciliation,

I couldn't take it, any more than I could take the pocket
    money he offered
the first ever.
'Go and buy yourself something nice.'

Too late,
And yet,
I have prayed and prayed for this moment,
scarcely believing, and cannot accept the gift,
the miracle,
this giant made man.
But a Father in heaven held out a hand to me
offering forgiveness, acceptance, reconciliation
and scarcely believing, I took it.
So, swallowing the bleak, fatherless years
which stick in my throat,
Slowly I reach out
and as finger touches finger
feel skin and bone, flesh and blood
and warmth
and for a few, fleeting hours
I am a daughter.

*Michele Guinness*
*(as recounted by Ann Needham)*


*Only in recent years has society acknowledged the injury
suffered by many women who have been sexually abused.
Recent surveys suggest that as many as 10% of women have
been abused as children, though not all are abused by their
fathers. Recovery from what journalist Tracy Hansen calls 'the
long reign of terror' can be a slow and frightening ordeal. It
may in fact be tempting to sit in the apparent safety of the*

*darkness, than strain for the pinprick of light at the end of the tunnel. But the same is true for each of us, abused or not, once we decide to let God confront us with our real selves.*

*'Angie' was abused as a child for many years by her father. She wrote these words after a great deal of counselling and prayer for healing.*


I have worn my ribbons and laces in all the right places.
Who dressed me?
Sad skies are opening my eyes
To the ribbons and laces,
hiding a face.
Take them away.
They lie.
Give them back to the father that never was
Who made me hide my face,
Behind the ribbons and lace.

My journey is long
My journey is slow
In search of reality
Because I am scared
Of the nakedness,
Behind the illusion
Of what everyone sees.

Only you know, God
that I am hiding my real face
which hasn't the grace
to be.
I have been living a lie
Till I dared to undress
And now you see

No ribbons and laces,
Only shame and nakedness,
You see me.

Tell me God, what do you see
When you look at the real me?
I tremble in my nakedness
You clothe me with your love
You hold me
And call me your child.
Yes, I have worn my ribbons and laces in all the right
   places
But when I chose to take them off
You made me go free.

*TRACY HANSEN was raped as a child by a close friend of the family. She repressed her trauma for more than thirty years, until one day the death-in-life experience of a survivor of child abuse became more than she could bear on her own. She told her story to a caring Catholic priest and that was the beginning of a slow and excruciatingly painful haul to wholeness.*

*She wrote this prayer in the midst of her trauma. 'As a result of using this prayer over a period of time, I began to feel compassion for adult survivors of child sexual abuse. I could not feel compassion for myself: I hated and blamed the "child within" for what she had been involved in, and despised the adult I had become. But expressing compassion for others who had suffered in a similar way was a first step in having compassion for myself and the child I had once been.'*

*Tracy is the assistant editor of* The Catholic Gazette *and also works as a translator.*

## Compassion

Jesus, our brother and friend
look with kindness and compassion
on those who were sexually abused.
You see the lost child within
still crying alone in the darkness
where the hidden wounds of childhood
still hurt, and make them afraid.
When they feel abandoned, give them hope,
when they feel ashamed, give them comfort,
when they feel unloved, give them faith,
when they feel betrayed, give them peace.

In the power of your resurrection
may love triumph over fear,
light shine in the darkness,
and the long reign of terror be ended.

*Tracy Hansen*

When I was a child I had a recurring nightmare. I dreamed that those I loved and knew suddenly had faces I didn't recognize, as if they were wearing masks. 'I don't know you', I said. But they laughed at my stupidity. And how it terrified me.

That nightmare became reality when you, beloved Dad, began to metamorphose before my very eyes. But in this case, I recognized your face, but not the person inside any more. 'You' disappeared somewhere behind the mask. And I was powerless to save you, to reach you, to bring you safely back. Alzheimer's Disease played foul, crept up from behind, used weapons and tactics I couldn't fight. You, who had always protected and defended me, said you would always be there for me, abandoned me, not in a moment, but little by little. Not as you used to pull the old sticking plasters from my cuts and grazes in one tear-jerking, hair-removing, sweep, as doctors do, but bit by bit, pulling and dragging and prolonging the agony.

Did you know how we nursed you and fed you and cared for you, you who had nursed and fed and cared for so many? I hope you didn't. I hope the disease was a little merciful, to you if not to us. For if you had known you would have fought, taken drastic measures to prevent the slow, sad destruction of so many proud, fine faculties.

I grieved as you died, year after year, until, when the final moment came, there were no more tears left. Not for you. Only for me, for I was vulnerable, defenceless, empty and fatherless.

97

With no one to shield me from my own mortality. I would want for nothing, you said, but now I want whenever I think of you, want your warmth and your humour, want your generosity and sense of fun, want your pride in your grandchildren and in me, for I never had time to show you how I would use all the riches you passed on to me.

'People must always come before principles, for without love people of principle are simply fanatics.'

'Do as you would be done by.'

'Balance in all things. Always examine both sides of the story.'

Simple, simple, homespun truths. But you lived them, and that's why I loved you. And therefore nothing was wasted, not even the end, when you were sweet and uncomplaining and accepting, as you always had been.

Strange, but now that you are gone I can get behind the mask and find you again, singing by my bed, accompanying yourself on the ukulele, jangling the coins in your pocket as we stopped at the sweetie shop on the way home from school, buying the teachers cream cakes on school sports days, playing cricket in the street, dancing the twist when it was the latest rage, savouring good red wine, admiring a fine pair of female legs. What a man you were!

I find you now in the words I speak, in the attitudes I adopt, in the goals I have, in the dreams you dreamed for me, so many of which have come true.

Most of all, I find you in the way I see God. And that has been the greatest gift of all.

*Michele Guinness*

# *Sisters!*

Sisters often have a love–hate relationship. Two women who owe their existence to the same source can be very similar or totally different, distanced or close, detached from each other or inseparable. The younger can be jealous of the older sister, the elder resentful of her younger sister.

Despite the sisterhood which seems to unite many women in their shared experiences, the blood relationship is not always so harmonious. Too much can be at stake, too many hurtful memories, too much vying for parental attention and affection. But when the relationship does fulfil its potential, it can be as fierce, as tender and as precious as any known to woman.

*REVD MAUREEN WITCOMBE is a deacon in the Sheffield diocese, married to an Anglican clergyman. She is also the Bishop's adviser on women's ministry. Her lot is not what her family would have expected of her. But then her sister surprised everyone too with her choice of career. In fact, Mo says, 'When my family realized I was heading for the ordained ministry and that my sister was a missionary their response was, 'Where did we go wrong?'*

We had a strange beginning. Our mother died when I was three and my sister was eight. She remained with our father. I, being so young and ill, was raised by my aunt and uncle. So we grew up apart, as 'only' children.

Living so far from each other, we met only once every two or three years. She used to love to say to people, 'My mother's sister is my sister's mother.' I idolized her. I was immediately attracted to anyone who looked like her and wanted to be like her. I failed, being so unsporty.

We wrote to each other often. Every letter was a treasure. And it was in her letters that she first hinted at her new faith. When the time came for me to be confirmed, it was she, now a student nurse in London, who explained the commitment I was about to make. And I understood.

We became 'double sisters', sisters in the spirit as well as the flesh, a special bond which has held us together, despite years of physical separation. For we were never destined to be together, have never lived anywhere near each other, never shared a Christmas together. She missed my wedding and the baptisms of our three children. Papua New Guinea is a long way away.

Yet the thread that binds us together cannot be broken. Our upbringing was totally different. We do not look alike, yet we have similar talents, similar gifts and a similar calling. We never cease to marvel at the closeness, though separateness, of our parallel paths, at the gift of our 'double sisterhood'.

*Maureen Witcombe*


## A Thousand Sisters

She climbed into the car with the burst of petrol bombs in
  her ears
And the image of a hundred soldiers on her mind,
    Just to get out, she thought,
    Anywhere . . . somewhere quiet

100

Somewhere the city lets its talon relax
to drop into silence,
Hear myself think –
Where God is.

The city limits welcomed her.
    'God – are you here?
    Where?
    Why are you not where people need you?
    Back there!
    Are you blind?'

God looked down at her then, with eyes,
    Eyes Christ had used
    That had looked down from a cross
    And saw – everything.

She tried to pray then, but fresh memories of mutilation
Burst onto her consciousness, and the city terror clung.
She tried to listen, but her legs ached with pain,
The pain of the memory of the bomb.

    'Be everywhere, Lord,
    BE! Hear . . . Answer the city
    Where people love and hate, pray and kill,
    Lord, this city has a thousand sisters
    Don't be deaf.
    DO something.'

She climbed into the car, watched the countryside retreat,
The city engulfed her, and God, hungrily
It's name was Belfast.
She passed waste ground where houses had been,
broken windows, burnt-out shops,

Washing beating against the wall, smudging chalk marks
   of hate,
Bitter slogans screamed at the car,
      And God spoke, quietly,
      'I see it
      Hear it
      Feel it
      Care,
      I have the answer.
      The power to stop it,
      The choice,
      is yours.
      Give me yourself
      LET me DO something.'

*Hilary McDowell*


## Sisters

Each new day yawns like an empty chasm
for the near-blind old woman
sitting in her little terraced house.

Ill-defined shapes people her world
dimly lit by the twice-weekly visit
of the paid home-help.

Some neighbours drop in to drink tea
and chat. Others do the shopping.
One, no longer welcome, looked round
at the cluttered chaos and said,
   'Couldn't live in a pig-sty.'

Her sister, Joan, eighty, but hale and hearty,
scolds her as she stumbles clumsily
round her shrunken room and says,
   'I don't know why you don't get dressed up
and go out. Look at me. I make the effort.'

One day, flustered by her sister's presence,
she blundered into a chair and fell down.
Joan made no move to help her to her feet
but said, 'By the way, we'd better discuss
it now. Do you want to be buried or cremated?'

*Hilda Cohen*

# Women and Sexuality

The Talmud, the commentary on the Jewish Law, states clearly that a God-fearing Jew should give his wife pleasure, particularly on the Sabbath. Nowhere does it say that he has a right to the same! Sadly, growing in a Greek culture as it did, the Church appears to have lost this positive, earthy approach to a woman's sexual needs, preaching a sub-conscious repression instead.

> You should not use outward aids to make yourselves beautiful, such as the way you do your hair, or the jewellery you put on, or the dresses you wear. Instead your beauty should consist of your true inner self, the ageless beauty of a gentle and quiet spirit, which is of great value in God's sight.

For generations of women in the Church, the apostle Peter's words have inhibited the full and free expression of their femininity. Nor has the early Church Fathers' condemnation of women as the gateway to destruction helped them to feel comfortable about their sexuality. For some, blending into the scenery, blandness and even dowdiness become qualities to covet. In others, sensual and sexual feelings have been ignored or feared. Until one day, as Anne Townsend discovered, the body refuses to be rejected a moment longer. The rays of the sun begin to thaw the ice. Then, gradually, beneath the warmth of the accepting smile of God, the ice melts and woman is born.

*R. S. THOMAS (b.1913) was Vicar of Aberdaron until he retired in 1967, three years after winning the Queen's Gold Medal for poetry. His experiences as the minister of 'large things in a small parish', striving to respond to the needs of the parishioners, examining his own faith and relationships in the light of social change, have always been at the heart of his writing.*

## The Woman

So beautiful – God himself quailed
at her approach: the long body curved
like the horizon. Why had he made
her so? How would it be, she said,
leaning towards him, if, instead of
quarrelling over it, we divided it
between us? You can have all the credit
for its invention, if you will leave the ordering
of it to me. He looked into her
eyes and saw far down the bones
of the generations that would navigate
by those great stars, but the pull of it
was too much. Yes, he thought, give me their minds'
tribute, and what they do with their bodies
is not my concern. He put his hand in his side
and drew out the thorn for the letting
of the ordained blood and touched her with
it. Go, he said. They shall come to you for ever
with their desire, and you shall bleed for them in return.

*R. S. Thomas*

*A missionary for many years, DR ANNE TOWNSEND discovered after an attempt to take her own life how negative she felt about herself, feelings compounded, not countermanded by her Christian faith. Her journey back to health and wholeness was a long and painful voyage of self-discovery, but as she neared the end of it, to her surprise, she was forced to confront her frozen sexuality, and, as she did so, she found herself blossoming both as a woman and as a child of God.*

Dear God

This will be hard to write since it's about something I'm used to being silent about – especially to you!

When I told you how my five senses have come alive so miraculously this summer, I didn't say anything about another awakening inside me. I've begun to notice delicious new, warm, good feelings that are part of my femininity – part of my sexuality. I find I'm rather ambivalent about them though. I realize that you created feelings like these and that they are good. But it's incredibly difficult not to follow the habits of a lifetime, on noticing such stirrings within me, and to catch and stifle them, deposit them in a black bin-liner (where they belong – don't they?) and trust the dustcart will have removed them by morning.

You know that in the past I would have couched this in virtuous, pious terms of 'fleeing lustful thoughts', 'avoiding temptation', or 'keeping myself pure for God'! However, there's a rebellious bit of me which I've not come across in the past. She screams in frustration: 'If they're good feelings, let them out, enjoy them, don't deny them life.' In the past I would have been concerned about this rebellious stranger. She might lead me astray. Today, I'm not too worried – after all, she has an important point, and between you and me, I think I rather like her!

So, this summer I have passed a peculiar milestone, haven't I, God? It's a milestone that I can tell you about, without feeling ashamed, that this summer I was able to relax fearlessly into my own sexuality, to explore some of its secret facets and to bask in its warmth and be tickled by its excitement. I even enjoy the programmes on television which I used to turn off (or watch hoping you and John wouldn't catch me)! I'm trying to get used to these feelings which haven't been part of my conscious self in the past – I know I would have felt ashamed, embarrassed and even in some ways sinful about them.

And God, I've got another bonus. Along with these warm, loving sexual feelings I'm enjoying, have come feelings about you. These days I tend to experience you just as if someone puts their arms round me and holds me tightly and lovingly. That's very good.

Good night, God. Love you!

*Anne Townsend*

*SISTER MARGARET MAGDALEN is the oblate sister of the Community of St Mary the Virgin in Wantage and has spent a number of years working in Africa. A religious community might not seem a likely habitat for a daughter of Overseas Missionary Fellowship parents and one-time member of the Baptist Church. But this rich blend of experience, her inner struggle for authenticity, in whatever tradition or environment she finds herself, seems to invest Sister Margaret's writing with an unusual dynamism and authority.*

*She is very concerned that single women should not be afraid to express their sexuality. Far from losing touch with her femininity and sexuality, she herself has found life as a Sister immensely liberating, perhaps because 'having taken vows of celibacy, everyone knows where we stand. I greatly enjoy the freedom to hug men without fear of giving the wrong signals.'*

108

One good reason for focusing on Mary Magdalen as an icon penetrating certain spiritual mysteries is that she succeeded where many of us fail. She seems to have reached an inner harmony where passion was converted or 'bridled by love', rather than denied, imprisoned, repressed or beaten out of the body (if that were ever possible!).

She who once used her earthiness in a way that dishonoured her sexuality, destroying true relationship and turning passion into lust, now allowed that same down-to-earthness to provide a channel for her love. The burning passion she now felt for Jesus *had* to find an outlet of expression . . .

Here was *pure* passion, fervent desire, expressed in a very overt, bodily contact, but untinged by lust, unspoiled by attention-seeking. For lust is always self-centred, greedy, grasping, out for its own ends, abusive and demeaning . . . It is dominated by the 'I want, therefore I must have' attitude, without thought or concern for those who are manipulated by its evil force . . .

So then, the energy of passion in Mary, which had previously been so foully misused and abused, is now converted. It does not lessen in power. Indeed, like channelling water, the diverting of it towards Jesus increases its power, for the love, which is reciprocated, is both life-giving and energizing.

In Christ all our lust can be taken up, converted, remade and transformed. Hence, Mary was free in herself to touch Jesus, weep over his feet, dry them with her hair, kiss them and anoint them.

Underneath the seemingly reasonable objections given by the onlookers, were these actions an uncomfortable evoking of memories for some of them? Did they find themselves recalling other occasions when *they* had been on the receiving end of similar treatment but in a very different context? Was it all a bit near the bone?

Whatever the reasons, they found Mary's behaviour absolutely shocking. What right had she to come barging in – on a male occasion – and force her attention upon Jesus, flagrantly performing an action which could have been, undoubtedly was, interpreted as full of sexual overtones.

But Jesus understood – completely. He knew the heart that motivated the action. He saw the purity of converted passion in Mary at that moment – a passion into which she could integrate her sexuality in a wholesome and holy way.

*Sister Margaret Magdalen CSMV*

*CHARLES KINGSLEY (1819–75), author of* Westwood Ho!, The Water Babies, *and many other well-known novels, was also Rector of Eversley in Hampshire, professor of modern history in Cambridge, a canon of Westminster Abbey and a celebrated preacher. The letters exchanged with his wife FANNY, both be-fore and after their marriage, reveal a passionate, sensual relationship and a strong erotic bond which continued through many years of married life.*

*It was stimulated perhaps by a long initial phase of self-denial. Determined to show both his beloved Fanny and God the depths of his self-control and purity, that his intense desire for his beloved's body was simply a reflection of his reverence for her soul, Kingsley asked her if she would be willing to remain a virgin for the first month of their marriage, so that when eventually they did lie naked in each other's arms, 'struggling, panting, dying for a moment', those 'thrilling writhings' would simply seem a foretaste of a more perfect union to come.*

*In fact they had many years to wait before they could test out his theory, years in which their Christian forbearance must have been pushed to the very brink, judging by the level of eroticism in the following two pre-marital extracts.*

## Charles to Fanny, 20 October 1843

What can I do but write to my naughty baby who does not love me at all and who of course has forgotten me by this time? But I have not forgotten her for my hands are perfumed with her delicious limbs, and I cannot wash off the scent, and every moment the thought comes across me of those mysterious recesses of beauty where my hands have been wandering, and my heart sinks with a sweet faintness and my blood tingles through every limb for a moment and then all is still again in calm joy and thankfulness to our loving God. Tomorrow I fast, not entirely, but as much as I can without tiring myself. Only to acquire self-control and to keep under the happy body, to which God has permitted of late such exceeding liberty and bliss.

## Fanny to Charles, 30 December 1843

After dinner I shall perhaps feel worn out so I shall just lie on your bosom and say nothing but feel a great deal, and you will be very loving and call me your poor child. And then you will perhaps show me your *Life of St Elizabeth*, your wedding gift. And then after tea we will go up to rest! We will undress and bathe and then you will come to my room, and we will kiss and love very much and read psalms aloud together, and then we will kneel down and pray in our nightdresses. Oh! What solemn bliss! How hallowing! And then you will take me up in your arms, will you not? And lay me down in bed. And then you will extinguish our light and *come to me*! How I will open my arms to you and then sink into yours! And you will kiss me and clasp me and we will both praise God alone in the dark night with his eye shining down upon us and his love enclosing us. After a time we shall sleep.

And yet I fear you will yearn so for fuller communion that

you will not be so happy as me. And I too perhaps shall yearn, frightened as I am! But every yearning will remind me of our self-denial, your sorrow for sin, your strength of repentance. And I shall glory in my yearning, *please God.*

*Passion of a kind the Kingsleys knew, continually stirred and stoked, can last well into later life. Or the embers may be left to die. The next two pieces, daughters' perceptions of their parents' love life, show that it can be a source of sadness – or hope – for the next generation.*

*ELIZABETH JENNINGS (b.1926) has been writing poetry since she was thirteen. What makes her different from her contemporaries, she says, is that she is a Roman Catholic, and a woman. Her faith, and her poetry, are the two most important things in her life.*

## One Flesh

Lying apart now, each in a separate bed,
He with a book, keeping the light on late,
She like a girl dreaming of childhood,
All men elsewhere – it is as if they want
Some new event: the book he holds unread,
Her eyes fixed on the shadows overhead,

Tossed up like flotsam from a former passion,
How cool they lie. They hardly ever touch,
Or if they do it is like a confession
Of having little feeling – or too much.
Chastity faces them, a destination
For which their whole lives were a preparation.

Strangely apart, yet strangely close together,
Silence between them like a thread to hold
And not wind in. And time itself's a feather
Touching them gently. Do they know they're old,
Those two who are my father and my mother
Whose fire from which I came, has now grown cold?

*Elizabeth Jennings*


## Sex For the Over-60s

Curved and companionable on the bathroom rack
two denture brushes lean against each other
my father and my mother.
Along the wet Llandudno sands
I watch them amble hand in hand
Dad natty in green slacks, and Mum
proud in her Marks and Spencers anorak;
and in the Boots bag I unpack
between the tissues and the Doggie Chox
a tube of lubricating gel
quietly in its quiet box
proclaiming all is well.

*Veronica Zundel*

# A Woman's Lot

A recent survey in a national newspaper discovered that though almost all men were glad they weren't women, 30 per cent of women would have preferred to have been born a man. A man is not subject to menstruation, the emotional see-saw of his hormones, the need to prove he can do a job, run a home and care for the children, all with a degree of perfection. He is not limited to the more menial tasks, seen as 'chattels' or a status symbol of middle-class affluence, patronized or seen to be perverse. How can woman fully identify therefore with a god who is seen to be male? How can she trust him if she isn't sure he really understands her?

The women who write here have found their status, their confidence and self-respect in the realization that God does know what they have to contend with, in the fact that they were given a major part to play in biblical history: 'First at the cradle, last at the cross.' If Christ treated them with nothing but courtesy and acceptance, how then dare men ignore or patronize them? At their peril, say Asian Christian women who are finding a voice at last.


CHRIST
How can you know a woman's grief?
The mother who watches her sons go to war
The bride who sees her husband
unemployed
empty in himself?

CHRIST
How can you know the boredom of a woman's mind?
The day to day battle with dirt,
Constant cleaning, washing
cleaning, washing
dirty socks, dirty floors?

CHRIST
How can you know the pain of a woman
The agony of children
The heaviness of heart when she sees her husband
drunk again
and ready for a fight?

CHRIST
How can you, God become man,
know these emotions?

CHRIST
Look to your mother
Look to her heartache
Her anxiety, her pain
and have pity.

*Amanda Swallow*

*LADY HOSIE was an Anglican laywoman and an ardent campaigner for the rights of women at the beginning of the twentieth century.*

*Both this short extract of her writing and Evangeline Booth's which follows it show that 'the Women's Movement' is by no means a new-fangled, seventies' or eighties' phenomenon.*

It is true that Jesus said greatly comforting things to women. He called a girl of twelve 'little darling', according to our new commentators, when he took her small hand and drew her back from death. He speaks to and of mothers and widows. He made no jokes about a mother-in-law, but raised one from her fever, and she ministered in the way that the mothers-in-law I know minister, even when dwelling in 'other people's houses'. I am not sure that the most beautiful story in the whole Testament is not that of the old woman, bowed these eighteen years in spirit and body, with no beauty surely on her face, and probably neither rich nor clever; yet one who had come to the place where she could meet with God. He had to 'call' her, for she would not think that a young man of three-and-thirty could seek out herself. But she was in need; and that was sufficient for the Good Shepherd.

The courtesy of Christ to women goes far deeper than race or appearance; and with that he has raised the nature of his fellow-men. Indeed, when I have heard good men tell an audience of women that they ought to be 'grateful' to Jesus, for he has 'raised the status of woman', I shrink, surprised by their blindness. It is just a century since slavery was abolished in the British Empire. Would we wish for our own sakes to go back to it, even if we could? Do we not pray to be delivered from the burden of knowing that some of our labour here is still semi-slavery? When we freed slaves, we ourselves were freed just as much as they.

*Lady Hosie*

*EVANGELINE BOOTH (1865–1950) was the daughter of William and Catherine Booth, the founders of the Salvation Army. All of the Booth daughters grew up watching their mother taking an equal lead in the Church, as popular a figure in the pulpit as her husband. Catherine believed that the influence of parents over their children 'is irresistible, until parents by their own injudicious conduct fritter it away'. Small wonder therefore that all her daughters grew up with a (before their time) vision of the role of women, both in their church and society, and with an intolerance of anyone who would waste time quibbling over the place of women, rather than rejoicing in every fighter for the gospel, male or female. Evangeline became the worldwide General of the Salvation Army in 1934.*

For what we call the women's movement is not social merely, not political merely. It is the direct fulfilment of the gospel of the Redeemer. It was Jesus who taught the world the full lesson of what is meant by chivalry to women. It was he who, at the well of Samaria, talked with an oft-divorced wife and told her of a God whom she could worship in spirit and in truth. It was he who, within the Temple itself, at Jerusalem, dared to defend a woman, taken in adultery, from her heartless persecutors by saying to a man in his hypocrisy, 'He that is without sin among you, let him first cast a stone at her.' He it was who visited the little girl on her deathbed and, by the omnipotence of love, called her back to life again. He it was who likened his Church to a bride, and himself to the bridegroom, drawing from the life of women, their lamps, their pieces of silver for housekeeping, the very broom with which they sweep the house, his immortal parables.

Happy, then, is the woman who realizes, even in these days of enfranchisement, that her life, however abundant it may be, is still hidden in the Christ of God. For it is in Christ that woman is transformed and transfigured by a miracle of redemption. Accustomed to flattery, to ease and to affluence, she breaks her alabaster box of spikenard, very precious, and pours the ointment over his feet, so that the fragrance thereof fills the whole house where they are sitting. Indeed, the woman who had nought save penitence to bring him, shed her tears also over those weary feet and wiped them with the hair of her head. Is it not the women who go to church? It has not always been so comfortable a place as church that women have trod the Via Dolorosa of a faith that nothing in heaven, nothing in hell itself could shake from its foundations. On that first Good Friday, when all the apostles had forsaken the crucified Christ and fled from the scene of his redeeming agony, it was the women who were last seen at the cross, watching him there; and on the morn of resurrection, when the night was still unlit by the first hint of the brightest dawn in history, the women were not afraid to risk the perils of those riotous streets and make their way, loyally and modestly and reverently, to the silent tomb. It was in the body of a woman that Christ was born; and the souls of women were the cradles of the Church.

*Evangeline Booth*

Perhaps it is no wonder that the women were first at the cradle and last at the cross. They had never known a man like this man – there never has been such another. A prophet and teacher who never nagged at them, never flattered them, never treated them either as 'The women, God help us!' or 'The ladies, God bless them!'; who rebuked without querulousness and praised without condescension; who took their questions and arguments seriously; who never mapped out their sphere for them, never urged them to be feminine or jeered at them for being female; who had no axe to grind and no uneasy male dignity to defend; who took them as he found them and was completely unselfconscious. There is no act, no sermon, no parable in the whole Gospel that borrows its pungency from female perversity; nobody could possibly guess from the words and deeds of Jesus that there was anything 'funny' about woman's nature.

*Dorothy L. Sayers*

119

*GODFREY HOLMES studied social sciences at university and went on to become a teacher. He had been head of the religious studies departments of two large comprehensive schools when he decided to retrain in counselling and social welfare. Since then he has worked in inner-city Nottingham as a specialist in fostering and adoption. He now lives in Chesterfield where he works with families at risk.*

## Men and Women

O God, women still fall so far behind men.
And girls fall so far behind boys.
Mothers suffer at the hands of fathers.
Schoolgirls stand around in corridors outside
watching schoolboys hogging computers inside.
Priests lead great religious processions
hardly noticing the women bringing up the rear.
Men deliver their speeches
refreshed by women laying on tea and cakes.
Managers still belittle manageresses.
Actors still upstage actresses.
Male sport fills every available television slot.
Whilst all the time
male moods attract fear and admiration;
female moods only attract pity and ridicule.
And when we address You, Our God.
we still talk in masculine terms –
Father, Almighty, King, Master of Mankind.
We said we'd aim for sexual equality . . .
so that women can do all the housework
and ask men to assist;
so that women can care for elderly folk
and ask men to stand by;
so that women can bring up the nation's children
and ask men to read them bedtime stories.

O God, help us to study our opposites
and to mean what we say about equal
treatment and equal treats.

*Godfrey Holmes*

*SANDRA HARGREAVES blames God and the monthly cycle for most of the trials of being a woman. A good moan with female friends and the occasional laugh about 'the curse of womankind' keeps us sane. But the poor old male of the species will never understand the amazing, unpredictable, hormonal roller-coaster which is his mate's monthly experience.*

## Pre-Menstrual Syndrome

I'm really feeling very stressed,
they put it down to PMS.
'A cup of tea is what I'd like,
Don't bother then! On your bike.
Sympathy and love, that's all I need,
Leave me alone, don't patronize me.
Why must you criticize all I do?
I'm sorry, my love, I do love you.'
I'm out of sorts and out of shape,
I'm all hemmed in, there's no escape.
Another broken cup, another slammed door,
I simply cannot stand any more.
You should experience this now and then,
You have it so easy, you lucky men.
I cannot help myself feeling blue,
Does no one love me after all I do?
I have no energy left, all I do is cry
and you just sit there wondering why.

121

Teenagers suffering from puberty
don't exactly blend with Mum's PMT.
What could possibly have been God's motive
to mix a family cocktail which is so explosive?
So please God help us through the years
Of frayed tempers, sulking and tears.
And we'll all survive as best we can.
Oh God, how I wish I'd been born a man!

*Sandra Hargreaves*

*In certain Christian denominations, and in other major world religions, women are still not allowed to take part in any of the important rituals, lest their monthly flow pollute the holiness of the occasion. GABRIELE DIETRICH, a German theologian living and teaching in South India since 1972, condemns this outrageous, outmoded attitude. For her, in imagery which is both shocking and stunning to our Western minds, menstruation is not a laughing matter, but a symbol of the Eucharist. Jesus bled on the cross, giving life to others. So women have been shedding their blood since eternity, in order to be a vehicle for new life.*

I am a woman
and my blood
cries out:
Who are you
to deny life-givers?
Each one of you
has come from the womb
but none of you
can bear woman

when she is strong
and joyful and competent.
You want our tears
to clamour for protection.
Who are you
to protect us
from yourselves?

I am a woman
and my monthly bloodshed
makes me aware
that blood
is meant for life.
It is you
who have invented
those lethal machines
spreading death:
Three kilotonnes of explosives
for every human being
on earth.

I am a woman
and the blood
of my abortions
is crying out.
I had to kill
my child
because of you
who deny work to me
so that i cannot feed it.
I had to kill my child
because i am unmarried
and you would harass me
to death
if i defy
your norms.

I am a woman
and the blood
of being raped
is crying out.
This is how you keep
your power intact,
how you make me tremble
when i go out at night.
This is how you keep
me in place
in my house where
you rape me again.
I am not taking this
any longer.

I am a woman
and the blood
of my operation
is crying out.
Even if i am a nun
you still use my body
to make money
by giving me a hysterectomy
when i don't need it.
My body is in the clutches
of husbands, policemen,
doctors, pimps.
There is no end
to my alienation.

I am a woman
and the blood
of my sacrifices
cries out to heaven.
I am sick of you priests
who have never bled

and yet say:
This is my body
given up for you
and my blood
shed for you
drink it.

Whose blood
has been shed
for life
since eternity?
I am sick of you priests
who rule the *garbagriha*
who adore the womb
as a source for life
and keep me shut out
because my blood
is polluting.

I am a woman
and i keep bleeding
from my womb
but also from my heart
because it is difficult
to learn to hate
and it might not help
if i hate you.

I am a woman
and my blood
cries out.
We are millions
and strong together.
You better hear us
or you may be doomed.

*Gabriele Dietrich*

*The following piece grew out of my reflections on what 'having it all' might mean for the Christian woman. Since there has been a tendency for the Church to rely on her being at home, so that she can provide the voluntary back-up so necessary to keep the machinery working, she may well find that she is under pressure to be the perfect church-worker, as well as the perfect wife, mother and colleague. Perfection however seems to elude human beings. Which means that working out our priorities, asserting our own autonomy, disappointing the expectations of others, is going to play a vital part in remaining sane and whole. After all, Jesus was the most assertive, integrated, holy human being who ever lived.*

I am that paragon of all paragons, that desire of governments and salvation of the nation: a woman returner; she who brings her wealth of accumulated wisdom and managerial expertise, gained through the nappy bucket and supermarket trolley, into that miniature democratic kingdom, the British work-place. This, so I'm told, is my moment of triumph, when, if it were not for fear of contravening the laws on sexual equality, countless employers everywhere, recognizing how invaluable our expertise, would be rushing to the job centres, and on bended knees demanding a female employee, married with at least six children. We can, we gather, dictate the terms, demand crèche facilities, have time off when the children are ill, synchronize our working hours with the school day.

But can we women really have it all: a career, a home, a husband, children, a dog, cat, budgie, leisure, peace of mind and the Church? Can we play the competent career lady with a well-groomed image, a dutiful wife with an hour-glass figure, a tireless church-worker with a disciplined spiritual life?

The new Christian woman must rise at six forty-five, shower, exercise and pray, set the breakfast table for her family, then, with curling tongs in one hand and mascara wand in the other,

126

prepare the evening meal, pop it in the oven or slow cooker, and set the timer so that it will be ready when everyone arrives home in the evening. She makes everyone their sandwiches, helps her husband to find his car keys, 'What, lost again, Dear?' and just remembers to feed the dog and put the cat out before she leaves the kitchen. She collects her papers together and puts them into her briefcase, along with the shopping list, so that in her lunch-hour she can just nip into the supermarket for those few rich-in-fibre commodities the family should eat fresh every day to keep them all regular in their habits.

By eight forty-five, singing a rousing chorus or two, she has braved the rush-hour traffic, dropped the kids off at school, returned home for a homework book left lying on the dining-room table, braved the traffic again, arrived at the office just in time to pre-empt the boss, organize his schedule, brief her colleagues, and make everyone their first cup of coffee of the day.

After several hours of answering the telephone, reorganizing a filing system which no one else respects, writing those urgent letters the boss was supposed to reply to last week and completely rearranging his schedule because of that dental appointment he forgot to put in the diary, she realizes it is twelve forty-five, collects her bags and heads for the nearest supermarket. But is intercepted by a colleague whose wife doesn't understand him. He talks and she responds with an hour or so of sympathetic nodding, watching the clock. Then completes the shopping in a record twenty minutes, manoeuvring her way through the check-out with the dexterity of a circus acrobat, praying all the while, of course, for her husband, the children at school, that the cat won't be run over, or the casserole overcooked, and for that colleague in need.

She is back in the office by two, reorganizes the filing system again, resolves a potentially lethal argument between two of the clerks, soothes ruffled feathers, massages hurting egos, clinches a couple of deals for the boss who's too unwell to do it himself after his dental treatment, rushes out to get him a couple of aspirin, finishes off a few more letters and memos, and arrives home just as the oven dings and the child minder is about to leave in a huff and never come back because little Jimmy has pasted the pages of her *Daily Light* together.

Her evening is divided between the work she brought home from the office, helping the children with their homework, ironing her husband's shirts, organizing a meeting of the local Neighbourhood Watch, and making a pizza or a quiche or both for tomorrow night's faith supper at church. At eleven she finally heads for bed, to sink into a well-earned stupor? Not a bit of it. This is the moment to don her baby dolls, say the experts, to make sure her marriage stays well and truly on the boil. Then, after a short prayer for the husband, the kids, the ageing parents, the faith supper and the unsaved masses, the lights go out and she sinks into glorious unconsciousness, sleeping the sleep of the righteous, for she is the quintessential new Christian woman.

*Michele Guinness*

*No section on the cost of being a woman would be complete without at least a passing acknowledgement of all we women suffer for the sake of beauty and fashion, in cultivating that accepted image of femininity imposed upon us by a multitude of cultural whims. And no matter how greatly the lady protesteth, the feminist burns her bra or refuses to shave her legs, the Christian decides to wear, or not wear a hat, paint her face, or be 'subject to the world', to stand against the tide like Canute requires enormous inner resolve and strength.*

*Scottish-born ELMA MITCHELL (b.1919) now lives in Somerset. She is a professional librarian who has also worked in broadcasting and publishing. She has published four collections of poems.*

128

## The Corset

The corset came today. I cannot wear it.

What are your difficulties, may I ask?
A slight constriction around the heart?
That, at your time of life, you must expect,
The back and shoulders mainly take the weight,
Astonishingly comfortable, on the whole
And really very stylish – for your size.
This line is very flattering to the bust,
And this delineates what once was a waist,
And further down, you see, complete control . . .

You'll soon acquire the knack; just slip it on,
Wriggle, distort, contract – that's right, that's it.
Now you are one smooth mould from head to thighs.
You'll be surprised how good it makes you feel . . .

The corset came today. I will not wear it.
Come, lumpish lumbering muscles, to your task,
Unsupple wits, turn sinuous again,
Or live as limp and cripple, but let live.

*Elma Mitchell*

# Woman At Work

My German sister-in-law, when she visited England for the first time, was very struck by the way the women she met talked of 'getting a job', rather than following a profession, having a career, or taking pride in their trade. At its very basic level a job is a job, a means of eating, staying alive. It is the daily grind promised to humankind by God when woman and man were banished from their garden paradise.

But there is another approach to work, to which Evelyn Underhill alerts us when she describes the potential of the teacher, which Jane Grayshon highlights when she analyses the difference a really good nurse can make. No matter how lowly, menial or treadmill, a job sanctified, made holy because we receive it as a gift from God, becomes a vocation. It is an opportunity to serve, a dirty word in our society. It is the opportunity to share the inner wholeness we have discovered, to take Christ out into the world and turn him into flesh and blood.

Women, who have traditionally taken the more caring or creative jobs, discovered this truth long before men. But the challenge is there to turn the most unlikely, routine occupation into a spiritual exercise.

But if that flickering spiritual motivation should be extinguished, how terrible is the inner darkness, for the job then becomes nothing more than a part to play, an empty shell void of the real woman.

131

*EVELYN UNDERHILL (1875–1941) is one of the best known mystics of the Church of England. She wrote extensively about mysticism and the spiritual life, and earned respect as a spiritual director and conductor of retreats at a time when few laywomen were deemed 'spiritual' enough to fulfil such a calling.*

## The Teacher

You, a child of God, are specially called upon to help and train the younger children of God to understand and deal with the rich and many-levelled life in which he has placed them: to educate them in the fullest, most profoundly Christian sense of that ill-used word. So a right attitude to him, the satisfying of your inner need of him, matters in your case supremely; not merely on account of yourselves and your own souls, but – which is much more important – on account of those who have been put in your charge, the little growing spirits for whom you are responsible to God. If that inner life goes wrong your work goes wrong.

A deep, wide and steady devotional life, pursued up hill and down dale, in darkness and in light, whether you feel like it or not, is therefore the essential foundation of your teaching work . . .

His interests are to be your interests, annihilating all concern with your personal status, personal success, personal preferences and aims. God will teach you, use you, support you – move, work through you – accepting you as one of his tools, part of his teaching apparatus. This position may or may not turn out pleasant for you. A real tool is seldom asked whether it cares to be used for a particular job or not. But unless you accept that situation with all that is implied in it, God is not going to accept you, use you and pour into your hearts something of his creative and enlightening love.

*Evelyn Underhill*

*Wearing 'the grinning mask of the minister's wife', hiding the real person behind the role, is an enormous pressure to bear. Unbearable if the gap between the woman and the role widens to such an extent that there seems little chance of ever integrating the two again. But it does happen, as this article which appeared in the* Guardian *on 7 May 1992 shows only too well.*

*Minister's wife or not, most of us struggle at home and at work to maintain our integrity, to resist the pressures which turn us into the high-powered career woman, the faithful church-worker, someone's wife, mum, colleague or teacher, to such an extent that our persona has little to do with the heaving mass of doubts, fears, worries which churn our inner selves, and are kept well hidden from those who could help us most.*

*But is being untrue to ourselves the cardinal sin? Are there not times when integrity itself might be nothing more than self-indulgent luxury? Is living a lie the easy option, or an act of supreme self-sacrifice?*

*This honest article, bearing the marks of intense pain and total exhaustion, raises many questions about these issues, and about the quality of the relationships we so often take for granted.*

Pardon my *cri de coeur*. After a couple of decades of life in a Nonconformist manse, I am not much given to crying or to unveiling my heart. The minister's wife, like Caesar's, needs not only to be above suspicion, but adept at concealing her own feelings while she lives publicly and often 'over the shop', smiling at the old ladies, befriending the young mums and putting Thomas the Tank Engine away in the church-hall engine shed after the crèche. Our church is, you must understand, a going concern. But that is not the only thing which is going, indeed gone. With a carelessness that might be considered catastrophic in a minister's wife, I have lost my faith.

I will not try to unravel the tangle of intellectual misgivings that have brought me to this point. Neither will I analyse whether the losing is of the 'gone for good' or the 'temporarily mislaid' variety. Please, Christian *Guardian* readers, do not, at this juncture, start praying for me. Without meaning to be ungracious, I can do without your prayers, as I am learning to do without my own.

Not surprisingly, after 30 years of energetic Christianity, this leaves me with a hole in my life. I could, I imagine, fill it with new people, old books and even older music. There is, however, a more pressing problem: faithless woman that I have now become, yet loyal wife, good mother and supportive friend that I still wish to be, what am I to do?

There are very real temptations (religious language is not easily unlearned), indeed sound reasons, for continuing to go through the motions of Sunday worship and business as usual in the church. Am I to scupper my husband's career by a resolute no-show in the pew? Make no mistake, a wife who does not attend church is not a professional asset for a clergyman. Less cynically, our whole relationship has been founded on a shared commitment to the life of the church.

What of my teenage children, one of whom is even now planning her annual visit to a Holy Day Camp where the 'Good morning, campers' will be superfluous for they will all have been engaged for hours in personal praise. Am I to imply that the faith which has served me well for 30 years may not similarly serve her? How can I hurt a couple of hundred church members who have never shown me anything but love?

It will not harm me, I tell myself, to continue to look after the tiniest in Junior Church on a Sunday morning, an exercise that has more to do with sticking and colouring and trips to the loo than it has to do with doctrine, and to continue to sing along on Sunday night. And is it really so hypocritical to continue to

134

work in church youth organizations? I am, after all, helping to offer a secure, user-friendly environment and a resource other than the television to the kids who live in the streets around the church.

In my brighter moments, I tell myself that it will not harm me to go through the motions. I know the motions and the words so very well. But in my darker moments I wonder what I may do to myself, my family, my friends – even to the child from an unhappy home who tells me, resting her head against me, that I am 'comfortable' – if I attempt to live however well-meaning a lie? Is personal integrity a pre-requisite for a sane and useful life? Or is it a selfish luxury few of us can afford to indulge?

Which way? Smiling on, concealing even from my nearest and dearest the confusion in what used to be my soul? Or some exceedingly painful nailing of my new colours to the mast? Pardon my *cri de coeur*. I am not much given to them.

### The Nurse

That nurse over there
    the one who is pouring a drink
    for the lady in the end bed
    whose thirst is never quenched –
She is the kind of person
Who gives the extra touches;
Nothing is too much for her.

    She chatters when she's bathing me
    Telling me of life outside these dreary walls.
    She listens when I talk to her
    Sensing when I need to laugh, to weep, to complain.

135

And when I'm sick
She lays her hand upon my brow
    with caring touch
    and soothing words
    and a cooling sponge
She wipes away gently the sweat of my exhaustion.

And when I've done
She lays me back upon soft pillows
Brushing my hair across fresh sweet-smelling whiteness
    away from my face
    away from my fears within.

And You, my God,
My Comforter –
You are the kind of person
Who gives extra touches;
Nothing is too much for You
No price too high.

    You poured out Yourself
    until You, too, knew the thirst
    which comes with dying.

When others give of themselves
They point me
To You.

*Jane Grayshon*

*SHEILA CASSIDY became headline news in 1975 when she was arrested and tortured in Chile for treating a wounded revolutionary.*

*After her horrendous experience she came home to Britain and entered a convent, but eighteen months later went back into medicine, the real love of her life. She now works at a hospice with cancer patients who are terminally ill.*

## The Carer

Slowly, as the years go by, I learn about the importance of powerlessness. I experience it in my own life and I live with it in my work. The secret is not to be afraid of it – not to run away. The dying know we are not God. They accept that we cannot halt the process of cancer, the inexorable march of that terrible army that takes over a human body like an occupying force, pillaging, raping, desecrating without respect and without quarter. All they ask is that we do not desert them: that we stand our ground at the foot of the cross. At this stage of the journey, of being there, of simply being: it is, in many ways, the hardest part.

*Sheila Cassidy*

# A Woman Spurned

For many years women have felt passed over by the Church. In the West, they have found themselves restricted to traditional female roles – cleaning the brasses, organizing the flower rota, running the Sunday School – long after society in general has begun to understand the folly of limiting the scope of a woman's potential. And though the historic decision of the General Synod of the Church of England of November 11th, 1992 to ordain women to the priesthood will go some way towards counteracting the sense of rejection many have felt over the years, women are still restricted in ministry and opportunity in certain other denominations, for example the Roman Catholic Church.

Asian women feel as rejected by the Church as their sisters in the West. Originally, they say, in the words of a Japanese poet, Hiratsuka Raicho, woman was the sun. An authentic person. But she has become the moon, 'she shines by reflecting', revolving around the sun. Now her struggle is to be the sun again.

Denial of gift, talent and potential has been a source of pain for women the world over, whether in the East or the West, and all agree that their greatest comfort is to see themselves reflected in God's, not man's eyes. For there they find acceptance, not rejection. For He is also She, who made women in Her image. He alone knows them well enough to make an honest, unbiased assessment of their gifts and ministry. He restores their long-lost authenticity, so that they can become the sun again, shining in its own light, fostering life in the Church and on earth.

*DOROTHY L. SAYERS (1893–1957) was most famous for the creation of her popular detective, Lord Peter Whimsey, a radically gentle, caring hero for the first half of the twentieth century.*

*She was highly educated for a woman of her era, having read modern languages at Somerville College, Oxford, but was rather a lone feminist voice in the Church of England, to which she was deeply committed. Her most famous work of Christian apologetics was the radio play,* The Man Born to be King, *broadcast by the BBC between 1941 and 1942. She also wrote the play,* The Zeal of Thy House, *which makes an unequivocal demand for women's gifts to be recognized, not spurned, and is included later in this anthology.*

There has never been any question but that women of the poor should toil alongside their men. No angry, and no compassionate, voice has been raised to say that women should not break their backs with harvest work, or soil their hands with blacking grates and peeling potatoes. The objection is only to work that is pleasant, exciting or profitable – the work that any human being might think it worth while to do. The boast, 'My wife doesn't need to soil her hands with work', first became general when the commercial middle classes acquired the plutocratic and aristocratic notion that the keeping of an idle woman was a badge of superior social status. Man must work, and woman must exploit his labour. What else are they there for? And if the woman submits, she can be cursed for her exploitation; and if she rebels, she can be cursed for competing with the male: whatever she does will be wrong, and that is a great satisfaction.

*Dorothy L. Sayers*

*A printed copy of this poem was sent to me, claiming that it had been written over 300 years ago, by a man, and a Catholic priest at that. This was wishful thinking! It was written in fact in 1979 by an American wife, mother and grandmother who had been concerned with the status of women in the Church and in society since early childhood, when second-grade girls tutored little boys in the Latin responses to the Catholic Mass, although they themselves were not allowed at the altar. It was sent by her sister to the* National Catholic Reporter, *who then published it, but had no idea where or how the strange story originated. But that in no way detracts from the power of its simple statement.*

Did the woman say
When she held him for the first time in the dark dank of a
    stable,
After the pain, and the bleeding and the crying,
    'This is my body, this is my blood'?

Did the woman say
When she held him for the last time in the dark rain on a
    hilltop,
After the pain, and the bleeding and the dying,
    'This is my body, this is my blood'?

Well that she said it to Him then,
For dry old men,
Brocaded robes belying barrenness
Ordain that she not say it for Him now.

*Frances Croake Frank*

*CHUNG HYUN KYUNG teaches theology at the Ewha Women's University in Seoul, South Korea. She electrified the 1991 World Council of Churches' Assembly in Canberra with her vivid presentation of Christianity in an Asian context. 'I approach Asian women's storytellings, poems and theological writings like a painter who is witnessing the eruption of a volcano', she says. Her mission in life is to make the world witness the explosion. Asian women will take their legitimate place in the Church once more. She sets out her challenge in* Struggle to Be the Sun Again, *a title drawn from a poem by the Japanese writer, Hiratsuka Raicho, which summarizes the aspirations of Asian Christian women everywhere.*

## The Hidden Sun

Originally, woman was the sun.
She was an authentic person.
But now woman is the moon.
She lives by depending on another
and she shines by reflecting
another's light.
Her face has a sickly pallor.

We must now regain our hidden sun.
'Reveal our hidden sun!
Rediscover our natural gifts!'
This is the ceaseless cry
Which forces itself into our hearts;
It is our final,
complete,
and only instinct
through which
our various
separate instincts
are unified.

*Hiratsuka Raicho*

142

*SUE MINTON lectures in psychology at the East Warwickshire College of Further Education in Rugby. She is also training to be a lay minister on the East Midlands Training Course, and in this capacity spends time with young offenders at Onley Prison. This meditation was written at an Ignatian retreat she attended, when she was invited to think herself into Mary's shoes. 'Taking her opportunities to minister where she finds them' is an important theme in Sue's life, for she finds herself denied the opportunities for which she had originally hoped.*

## One Woman's Ministry

Martha and Mary were second-class citizens,
Being mere women in a male-dominated society.
Mary sat passively at the feet of Jesus,
And the disciples tolerated her there,
The position symbolizing her inferiority.
Mary didn't waste time in resentment,
Nor in arguing her equality –
She took her opportunities where she found them
And, since she was at foot level,
Expressed her love for Jesus through his feet.

There's something very intimate about feet;
What a privilege to minister to the feet of God,
Smoothing in ointment with gentle fingers!
Did the disciples notice her at first?
They were probably jostling for status.
Mary knew her value,
And it wasn't their assessment of her!
So, when her brother died,
And Jesus wept with her in mutual grief,
I think he cried in her arms.

*Sue Minton*

143

*EDWINA GATELEY was born in Lancaster into a Catholic family. Following her work in Uganda as a teacher and her founding of the Volunteer Missionary Movement in 1969, she took a degree in theology and wrote the much-acclaimed* Psalms of a Laywoman.

*But then her life changed course, dramatically. It began with a nine-month stay in a hermitage in the forest in Yorkville, Illinois, 'trying to get in touch with myself as a woman, trying to be still and to listen to the God within me'. What God revealed to her was his immense love for all humanity, particularly those who hurt the most.*

*This time of profound silence culminated in a thirty-day retreat, where she received the clear call to go out and act upon the revelation she had received. She writes:*

> *I was always curious about prostitutes. I wondered why women prostituted themselves. I came to realize that my own experience as a woman and in particular, as a Catholic woman in a male-controlled, authoritarian church, has not been, like it or not, without its prostituting moments. I became more aware of how all women are inevitably conditioned to sell themselves one way or another, whether it is for approval, acceptance, love, security, or, indeed, money. The very nature of our patriarchal society produces prostitutes – and pimps.*

*Out of her work with prostitutes on the streets of Chicago has grown Genesis House, a haven for anyone seeking to escape to the new, 'caring, compassionate, world . . . where there will be no more victims and abusers, but only sisters and brothers on God's holy mountain'.*

## The Anointing

There were no crowds at my ordination,
The church was cold and bare,

There was no bishop to bless and consecrate,
No organ music filled the air.
No solemn procession went before me,
No cross or incense smell,
There were no songs nor incantation
And no triumphant, pealing bell.

But I heard the children laughing
In the stench of the city slums.
And I heard the people sobbing
At the roaring of the guns.
And the stones cried out before me
As the sirens wailed and roared
And the blood of women and children
In the arid earth was poured.

There were no crowds at my ordination,
The church was cold and bare.
But the cries of the people gathered
And the song of birds filled the air,
The wind it blew cold before me,
The mountains rose and split,
The earth it shuddered and trembled
And a flame eternal was lit.

There were no crowds at my ordination,
The church was cold and bare,
But the Spirit breathed oh, so gently
In the free and open air,
She slipped through the walls and the barriers,
And from the stones and the earth she proclaimed:
Oh, see! My blind, blind people,
See woman – whom I
Have ordained.

*Edwina Gateley*

# *Where Women are Powerless*

If comparatively affluent women in the West often feel scorned and spurned, helpless and powerless, how much more is that true of our sisters throughout the world, who because of geography, poverty, famine, culture, upbringing or prejudice, find themselves trapped, without status, without a voice. Such is their suffering that sometimes all we can do is sit with them in a symbolic way, offering them in our silence, our identification with them in their pain, some small kind of loving support and understanding. At other times anger converts the silent intercession into a volcanic torrent. Some, like Edwina Gateley, have been called away from private prayer, to intercede in a more physical sense, to be 'God on the streets of Chicago'.

But always the lives of countless women, suffering and oppressed, call us out of our own complacency, challenge us to look beyond our own private struggle for authenticity, make us aware of the special experiences which make women unique and bind us together, beyond the boundaries of culture and continents, into one sacred sisterhood.

### Intercessions

I come to intercession Lord, and this the hardest of all.
Before I begin I am filled with shame and despair;

147

Shame, because I, who have so much, have given so little;
Despair, because there are so many people, so many
  problems
Can these thoughts I offer you really make any difference?

How can I know the feelings of those whose handicapped
  bodies make a cage without a door?
How can I understand the loneliness of the unloved or the
  mentally ill?
What comprehension can I, cocooned in my soft bed,
  have of the agony of giving birth on the hard earth?
Or the bitterness of a mother having only a milkless
  breast to offer her child?

I watch the endless procession of faces on the screen,
What can they know of your love and glory?
But it is the faces of the children what always start my
  tears.
I want to turn away but I know that you want me to see.

*Joan Pluciennik*


## God In the Brothel

I went to the brothel
and took God
with me.
The Madam cursed and spat
fury and hatred,
spewing it out
all over the kitchen
and all over God.

The girls sat listless,
in dreadful despair,
waiting for customers,
with their dirty minds,
and cold, cold lust.
The men,
furtive and awkward,
in their smart business suits,
itching to rape,
and to steal
before driving home
to the wife and kids,
and barbecue
on the lawn.
I went to the brothel
and found God
within.
And, through all
the sickness,
the sin, and
the stink,
God sat,
in stunned and dreadful
silence.

*Edwina Gateley*

*This poem was inspired by the suffering of a black woman in South Africa.*

## Tribal Burial

See that man
in the grey speckled blanket?
He's mine.

Others wore blankets
of sand-coloured, mud-coloured
brown.
Mine wore grey flecked
with white, like birds' feathers.

They used to come striding
home, up the hill paths,
bringing their wages,
mine in his speckled grey.
I could see him coming.

There they lie, now,
in a row, eight of them,
wrapped head to foot
in sand-coloured mud-coloured
brown.

That one in the speckled grey,
he's mine.

*Evangeline Paterson*

*SOJOURNER TRUTH (1797–1883) was the name adopted by the slave, Isabella, when the New York Emancipation Act gave her freedom in 1827. In 1843, with 25 cents and a bag of clothes, she set out to travel the coast singing and speaking about slavery and women's rights. Tall, witty and dramatic she was a source of fascination to white audiences, but the main work of her life, a petition on black land ownership, lay gathering the dust on a Congress shelf. This famous speech of hers was set out as poetry by Erlene Stetson.*

### Ain't I Woman?

That man over there say
    a woman needs to be helped into carriages
and lifted over ditches
    and to have the best place everywhere.
Nobody ever helped me into carriages
    or over mud puddles
        or gives me a best place . . .

And ain't I woman?
    Look at me
Look at my arm!
    I have ploughed and planted
and gathered into barns
    and no man could head me . . .
and ain't I woman?
    I could work as much
and eat as much as a man –
    when I could get to it –
and bear the lashes as well
    and ain't I woman?

I have borne thirteen children
    and seen most sold into slavery
and when I cried out a mother's grief
    none but Jesus heard me . . .
and ain't I woman?
    that little man in black there say
a woman can't have as much rights as a man
    'cause Christ wasn't a woman
Where did your Christ come from?
    From God and a woman!
Man had nothing to do with him!
    If the first woman God ever made
was strong enough to turn the world
    upside down, all alone
together women ought to be able to turn it
    rightside up again.

*Sojourner Truth*

# Women of Courage

Courage has traditionally been a male attribute. Little boys have been taught not to cry and to be brave much more often than little girls. But from the beginning of time women have shown themselves to be resilient and strong, capable of acts of extraordinary courage. 'It's too late to frighten a woman with risks', says Ursula in Dorothy Sayers' *The Zeal of Thy House*. Eve, the first woman, took the first risk when she handed Adam the fruit, and women have ventured all ever since. For many centuries childbearing itself was a risk, but that never prevented women from playing with their lives to continue the human race. And some would say that it is this capacity to give and protect life which can make women more daring than men. Some, like Florence Nightingale, would say it is because they have been denied so much that they have learned to fight the harder.

All the women whose experiences are recorded here, whether in prison or concentration camp, fighting God, the Church or the System, confronting prejudice, oppression or the toughest enemy of all, death, have discovered inner resources they never knew they possessed. Faith arms them with super-human courage.

*Your old men shall dream dreams, and your young men see visions – but not your women.' So says William, the architect, in Dorothy Sayers' play* The Zeal of Thy House, *as he explains*

*to Ursula why she cannot play a part in his magnificent*
*obsession to build the greatest cathedral of all time. She*
*responds:*

I understand.
Knowledge and work – knowledge is given to man
And not to woman; and the glory of work
To man, and not to woman. But by whom
Came either work or knowledge into the world?
Not by the man. God said, 'Ye shall not know;
Knowledge is death.' And Adam was afraid.
But Eve, careless of peril, careless of death,
Hearing the promise, 'Ye shall be gods',
Seized the knowledge for herself, and for the man,
And all the sons of men; knowledge, like God;
Power to create, like God; and, unlike God,
Courage to die. And the reward for her
Was sorrow; But for Adam the reward
Was work – of which he now contrives to boast
As his peculiar glory, and in one breath
Denies it to the woman and blames her for it,
Winning the toss both ways. My simple Adam,
It is too late to scare woman with risks
And perils – woman, that for one splendid risk
Changed the security of Paradise,
Broke up the loom and pattern of creation,
Let in man's dream on the world, and snatched the torch
Of knowledge from the jealous hand of God
So that the fire runs in man's blood for ever.

*Dorothy L. Sayers*

*DAVID MICHELL was born in China, the son of missionary parents. In 1942, when he was only eight years old, the Japanese invaded the China Inland Mission school he was attending at Chefoo in north-east China, and took all the staff and pupils to the Weihsien concentration camp.*

*The children were separated from their parents for several years, and the teachers did their best to spare them the worst of the trauma, disease, misery and malnutrition. They endeavoured not only to make the camp as bearable an environment as possible for the children, but even to create an atmosphere of celebration when the occasion demanded it. Such as the day on which two of the staff were married. Beatrice Lack was the school cook. The effort, recorded in her diary, to make the wedding cake is a tribute to the unquenchability and ingenuity of the female spirit, even under extreme pressure.*

*It was at Weihsien Camp that the Olympic athlete and missionary, Eric Liddell, would die at a tragically young age of a brain tumour before the end of the war.*

## Mrs Lack's Cake

We made up our minds that as the cake was about all we could give, we would give our best. One hundred and fifty guests were invited, including all children in the Senior School . . . Everyone made contributions. I also collected apricot stones from people who had been fortunate enough to get a few apricots, and these made lovely almonds. Also bits of orange and pumelo skin, some nearly two years old, were added. It grated up beautifully and gave the flavour which was all that mattered. We managed to collect two pounds of sugar altogether for this special cake, using a quarter of it for the cake and the rest for icing purposes. With a few real sultanas from our Red Cross parcels and a little dripping given me from one of the kitchens, plus oddments of spice and cinnamon, we

155

set about this cake-making with a professional feeling. Lots of Chinese dates helped to make the mixture sweet. The tins were anything except cake tins, but we managed to get three sizes of right proportions, including a powdered milk tin for the top tier. The baking took five hours in a kerosene tin oven. The decorations were made from silver paper or tin foil. The pillars of wood were covered with tin and then polished. Someone lent a cake icing outfit and with some persistence we managed to make a boiled icing work for decorations. The ornament on the cake, a Gothic arch, I made from a strip of tin released on opening a tin of milk. This was covered with white tape and lily-of-the-valley (a bunch of artificial flowers I had worn for five summers), with little bits of green here and there and with little bells hanging on the top gave it the finished look. The children loved preparing for the wedding, and we all looked upon it as a jolly good excuse for a cake.

*CORRIE TEN BOOM was still a young woman when the Nazis invaded her native Holland. One of two unmarried daughters of the local watch repairer, she had led a sheltered life, but her Christian conscience would not let her stand by and watch the destruction of the Jewish community. She hid many Jews in her home and eventually, after several years, she and the rest of her family were caught and taken to Ravensbruck, where Betsie her sister died. Corrie survived and travelled the world, speaking about her rich experience of God's faithfulness, even in times of immense horror and suffering.*

It was in a church in Munich that I saw him, a balding heavy-set man in a grey overcoat, a brown felt hat clutched between his hands. People were filing out of the basement room where I had just spoken, moving along the rows of wooden chairs to the door at the rear. It was 1947 and I had come from Holland to defeated Germany with the message that God forgives.

It was the truth they needed most to hear in that bitter, bombed-out land, and I gave them my favourite mental picture. Maybe because the sea is never far from a Hollander's mind, I liked to think that's where forgiven sins were thrown. 'When we confess our sins,' I said, 'God casts them into the deepest ocean, gone forever.'

The solemn faces stared back at me, not quite daring to believe. There were never questions after a talk in Germany in 1947. People stood up in silence, in silence collected their wraps, in silence left the room.

And that's when I saw him, working his way forward against the others. One moment I saw the overcoat and the brown hat; the next a blue uniform and a vizored cap with its skull and crossbones. It came back with a rush: the huge room with its harsh overhead lights, the pathetic pile of dresses and shoes in the centre of the floor, the shame of walking naked past this man. I could see my sister's frail form ahead of me, ribs sharp beneath the parchment skin. Betsie, how thin you were!

Betsie and I had been arrested for concealing Jews in our home during the Nazi occupation of Holland; this man had been a guard at Ravensbruck concentration camp where we were sent.

Now he was in front of me, hand thrust out: 'A fine message, Fraulein! How good it is to know that, as you say, all our sins are at the bottom of the sea!'

And I, who had spoken so glibly of forgiveness, fumbled in

my wallet rather than take that hand. He would not remember me, of course – how could he remember one prisoner among those thousands of women?

But I remembered him and the leather crop swinging from his belt. It was the first time since my release that I had been face to face with one of my captors and my blood seemed to freeze.

'You mentioned Ravensbruck in your talk,' he was saying. 'I was a guard in there.'

No, he did not remember me.

'But since that time,' he went on, 'I have become a Christian. I know that God has forgiven me for the cruel things I did there, but I would like to hear it from your lips as well. Fraulein' – again the hand came out – 'will you forgive me?'

And I stood there – I whose sins had every day to be forgiven – and could not. Betsie had died in that place – could he erase her slow terrible death simply for the asking?

It could not have been many seconds that he stood there, hand held out, but to me it seemed hours as I wrestled with the most difficult thing I had ever had to do.

For I had to do it – I knew that. The message that God forgives has a prior condition: that we forgive those who have injured us. 'If you do not forgive men their trespasses,' Jesus says, 'neither will your Father in heaven forgive your trespasses.'

And still I stood there with the coldness clutching my heart. But forgiveness is not an emotion – I knew that too. Forgiveness is an act of the will, and the will can function regardless of the temperature of the heart. 'Jesus help me!' I prayed silently. 'I can lift my hand. I can do that much. You supply the feeling.'

And so woodenly, mechanically, I thrust my hand into the one stretched out to me. And as I did, an incredible thing took place. The current started in my shoulder, raced down my arm, sprang into our joined hands. And then this healing warmth seemed to flood my whole being, bringing tears to my eyes.

'I forgive you, brother!' I cried. 'With all my heart!' For a long moment we grasped each other's hands, the former guard and the former prisoner. I had never known God's love so intensely as I did then.

*Corrie Ten Boom*

*There is a tendency among women to take the blame, even when a particular situation is not our fault. We take upon ourselves all sorts of guilt which does not belong to us, possibly because our upbringing tells us that it is the nice, female thing to do, possibly because we simply haven't got the time to think up excuses the way men do.*

*But when PAM CAVENDISH was involved in a horrendous car crash, as she tried to come to terms with the shock of it she discovered that taking the blame was not the best way to rediscover her equilibrium. There had to be a more whole, helpful and courageous way out of the personal crisis.*

I've never been a screamer. When heroines in films let out an ear-piercing belter, I've always thought, 'I could never do that'. As a child I would never scream with fright when chased by the boys. I would just go silent. I could never even replicate the tiniest beginnings of a scream under the bedclothes. Any attempt at noise would always seem clumsy and inadequate. My screams were always pushed well down, way beneath the surface of my serene existence.

Then one day I heard myself scream and since then I've never really stopped. I was in a car crash. A head-on collision.

There was just enough time to register what was about to happen. And I screamed. From the depths. With all my strength. And I remember thinking, 'Where is all that noise coming from?'

I was badly hurt and it took months to recover. The mental damage took even longer to repair. Whenever I thought about the accident, the tears welled up inside. Surely I was to blame. Everyone, witnesses, police, friends said not. But I knew I must take the blame, the hurt, the pain, all of it, and cry quietly as I had always done. But this was too big. The violation too great. The scars obvious every time I looked in the mirror.

I had been hurt and someone else was to blame.

My next scream was deliberate. I climbed into our airing cupboard, buried my head in the clothes inside, and said through the tears, 'You've hurt me.' This time I didn't swallow hard. I let the scream come. It wasn't as loud as I might have liked. But it was my scream. A scream from inside which said, 'I'm hurt and you caused it, and if you were here you'd hear my scream and you'd know that too.'

That unlocked the doors. I don't scream all the time. But I know I can if I need to. I can now allow myself to feel pain, rather than absorb it. Then I can have done with it. Memories, many painful memories from the past, have flooded back since that day in the airing cupboard, and stand in a queue, waiting to be screamed at. In a very real way I know now that my screaming will never stop.

*Pam Cavendish*

*MARY CRAIG's second child, Paul, was born with gargoylism, a rare disease which leaves the victim physically impaired and mentally retarded. Overwhelmed by the pressures of caring for a child too handicapped even to recognize her, she was all but crushed, until she found herself volunteering to work for a week at a home for disabled Nazi concentration camp survivors. Amazingly, it was there, amidst people horribly maimed yet still courageous and cheerful, that she found the strength to accept her life. When her fourth child was born with Down's Syndrome she had learned how to bear this second terrible blow.*

What did we really feel when Paul died – this child of ours who had never even recognized us? I can only speak for myself, and admit to a confused complexity of emotions. I knew that Paul's death was a release for all of us, and there is no denying that I felt a deep thankfulness that this phase of my life was over. But I felt grief too, most probably for the loss of the child he might have been; and there was the even greater pain of believing that I had failed him. A kind of desolation swamped me for a time, and for nights on end I could do nothing but cry. It was a crying which had no rationale except in remorse, and in some odd way I felt I was not entitled to genuine grief. Our friends were so sure that Paul's death was an unqualified blessing that I felt guilty about the grief I felt for him. I knew that what hurt most in the general rejoicing was the assumption that Paul's life had been a useless irrelevance, a disaster best forgotten.

To me it did not seem like that. Yes, I was glad he was dead. But at the same time I owed him an incalculable debt. If our value as human beings lies in what we do for each other, Paul had done a very great deal: he had, at the very least, opened the eyes of his mother to the suffering that was in the world, and had brought her to understand something of the redemptive force it was capable of generating. I had been broken, but I had been put together again, and I had met many who bore far more inspiring witness than I to the strength

161

inherent in the mending process. What Paul had done for me was to challenge me to face up to the reality of my own situation; and he had handed me a key to unlock reserves buried so deep I hadn't suspected their existence.

He had taught me a lesson, quite unwittingly, and now that he was no longer there, I owed it to him not to forget.

*Mary Craig*

*IRINA RATUSHINSKAYA (b.1954) was only 28 years old when the Soviet system sentenced her to seven years' hard labour for 'the manufacture and dissemination of poems'. It was the culmination of years of rebellion against a system which negated her right to believe and to express that faith in writing. She nearly died from maltreatment in the camp, which was reserved for 'especially dangerous' criminals, and it was only due to worldwide protest following the leaking of her poems to the West that she was freed in 1986.*

I sit on the floor, leaning against the radiator –
A southerner, no-gooder!
Long shadows stretch from the grating, following the
    lamp.
It's very cold.
You want to roll yourself into a ball, chicken-style.
Silently I listen to the night,
Tucking my chin between my knees.
A quiet rumble along the pipe:
Maybe they'll send hot water in!
But it's doubtful.
The climate's SCHIZO. Cainozoic era.
What will warm us quicker – a firm ode of Derzhavin,

162

A disfavoured greeting of Martial,
Or Homer's bronze?
Mashka Mouse has filched a rusk
And is nibbling it behind the latrine pail.
A two-inch robber,
The most innocent thief in the world.
Outside the window there's a bustle –
And into our cell bursts =
Fresh from freedom –
The December brigand wind.
The pride of the Helsinki group doesn't sleep –
I can hear them by their breathing.
In the perm camp the regime's
Infringer doesn't sleep either.
Somewhere in Kiev another, obsessed,
is twiddling the knob of the radio . . .
And Orion ascends,
Passing from roof to roof.
And the sad tale of Russia
(Maybe we are only dreaming?)
Makes room for Mashka Mouse, and us, and the radio set,
On the clean page, not yet begun,
Opening this long winter
On tomorrow.

*Irina Ratushinskaya*


*In 1852 Florence Nightingale wrote, to her friend Dean Stanley,
her thoughts about the Church of England. 'I would have given
her my head, my hand, my heart', she wrote, 'but she told me
to go back and to crochet in my mother's drawing-room. "You
may go to the Sunday School if you like", she said. But she*

163

*gave me no training even for that. She gave me neither work to do for her, nor education for it.'*

*Many women over the centuries have been forced to follow their destiny and exercise their gifts without the support of their Mother Church, indeed, sometimes despite and in direct contravention of it. That can be a fearful prospect, but the issue, the vision, is not merely self-fulfilment, a paltry and rather questionable goal for the Christian, but rather the advancement of the kingdom of God itself.*

*MARY STOCKS, born in 1891, was the Principal of Westfield College, a frequent broadcaster, a fighter for women's suffrage, outspoken in the promotion of the welfare state, and a pioneer in advocating birth control. She was made Baroness Stocks in 1966.*

We acquired two rooms in a working-class area, found a woman doctor bold enough to officiate, and two nurse-midwives bold enough to assist her, and in 1925 opened what I think was the first provincial birth-control clinic.

Our premises were in one respect fortunately situated; for they were on an upper floor, approached through a shop which sold meat pies. This meant that shy clients were not readily identifiable from the street as visitors to the clinic – they might equally well be regarded as pie purchasers. In another respect we were less fortunately placed, because our clinic was in the near neighbourhood of a large Roman Catholic church, and officially Roman Catholics did not like us at all. Indeed, they did all they could to frustrate our venture; even to the extent of organizing a huge protest meeting at which one speaker accused us of practising abortion. The result of this meeting was not, however, all that its promoters could have wished; because for some time after its occurrence our routine question, 'How did you hear of the clinic?' might provoke the answer, 'At the protest!'

On one occasion Charis Frankenburg and I found ourselves described in a Roman Catholic publication as 'the kind of idle women who visit matinees and sit with cigarettes between their painted lips'. This image of ourselves afforded us some pleasure because we were apt to envisage ourselves as rather dowdy social workers. On another occasion the access to our clinic was described as 'through a stinking entry'. This was a half-truth, because though a potent aroma certainly followed one up its staircases, it was a pleasant and comforting aroma of freshly cooked meat pies.

In view of authoritative Catholic doctrine, the attitude of our local Roman Catholic clergy was easy to understand. Less easy to understand was the non-committal but on the whole hostile aloofness of the Anglican Church. In many clerical minds, and indeed many other minds, birth-control was associated with irregular sex relations, as indeed it well may be. It was also, in those far-off days, associated with strange myths which we often encountered and, as time went on, were able to dispel; for instance that it caused cancer, or that once practised, it produced subsequent sterility.

*Mary Stocks*

*DEACONESS PHOEBE WILLETTS (1917–78) must have been one of the most extraordinary church women of the 1960s and 70s, the female equivalent of 'a turbulent priest', a thorn in the side of both the spiritual and political establishments. An outspoken advocate of nuclear disarmament, she served a six-month prison sentence when her children were teenagers, for sitting in the entrance of Foulness atomic weapons research establishment. 'If you believe something has to be done,' she said quite simply, 'you do it.'*

165

*She campaigned for the admission of women to the
priesthood of the Church of England at a time when few were
doing so. She and her husband, Alfred, invited the American
woman priest, Alison Palmer, to be the first woman to celebrate
the Eucharist in a Church of England parish church. It caused
quite a furore in the Church establishment. Phoebe failed to
tell her bishop that she was dying of cancer at the time, 'so that
he could give us as big a row as he wanted'.*

*Later, when she knew the end was very near, her husband
wheeled her into their Manchester church where they
concelebrated the Eucharist together, the first such celebration
in the Church of England. It was to be the culmination of her
entire ministry, one she had shared with her husband
throughout their married life and a fitting final gesture for
someone who had fought so hard for women to be given equal
status and opportunity to serve with men in the Church.*

## Woman's Cry of the Heart

Dear God,
make a full and complete woman of me,
not an also ran or a pale reflection of a man
included in that word: 'man'.
The men say, 'Jesus died for us men and for our salvation'
as if I were part of a package deal,
part of his household, his luggage:
but I know I am not just a part of his equipment to be a
    person.
I am an other, quite different person.

I have my own name,
my own personality.
I am feminine
and that is quite different from being masculine.

166

I don't want to be a secondary part of a man.
I want to stand opposite him,
straight and tall,
to look him in the face as my equal.
I want to help him.
I can't help him unless I am allowed to think for myself
and challenge him.
I want to help men to see they have been created
artists, poets and prophets,
not fighters and killers:
not destroyers, but builders.
I am their priest.
You have called me to prophesy to them.

The word of the Lord came to me saying
'Go and prophesy to your brothers.
Tell them they must lay down their sword and spear,
their bombs and deterrents
and publish tidings of Peace from the mountain tops.
They must learn to sit at the feet of their mothers and
    wives,
sisters and daughters,
learning the ways of tenderness and compassion,
the lessons tiny children can teach them.'

Lord, help me to know I am a priest
whether man's-church recognizes it or not.
Help me to know that women were ordained priest at
    Pentecost:
that your Holy Spirit was given to the women
as well as the men,
that no man can ever take that from me.

Help me to love men enough to stand up to them,
challenge their way of running the world,
their way of running the Church.
Help me to rid them of pagan militarism
which Constantine let flood into the Church.
I know I could not have gone to bed with a fighter or
  killer.
I could not have waved a man off to war.
Jesus showed us another way of standing up to evil.
He showed us it is better to die than kill.
He showed us the way of suffering love,
the brave man's choice.

He it is who can make it possible
for Woman the Priest and Man the Builder, Poet and
  Prophet
to build a better world
fit for our granddaughters.
I have three granddaughters.
I am glad they are granddaughters
for to them belongs the future.
Women must discover their identity in Christ,
a glorious vision lying in wait for them to unwrap,
like a beautiful birthday present.

*Phoebe Willetts*

*Many may teach us how to live, but few teach us how to die. Yet it is a transition we will all have to make one day, and how much the harder when there are children and other loved ones to leave behind.*

*ROSIE HOPPER (1946–91) was propelled into writing when she discovered that her end was imminent. Married in 1970, the mother of three children and a nurse, she was first diagnosed as having cancer in 1978. The secondaries did not appear until the autumn of 1989, giving her about ten relatively problem-free years in between.*

*Rosie's winding, rather tortuous spiritual journey took her from an Anglo-Catholic junior school, via the 'Navigators' when she was a student nurse, into charismatic Anglicanism, while she and her husband Richard were House Wardens of the Lee Abbey Students' Club in Earls Court. Several years in the mainstream of the Church of England led into a spiritual wilderness, until, in 1985, she joined the Quakers and felt as if she had come home. The Quaker women's group she attended fortnightly for silence and sharing was a safe haven, somewhere to share her struggles, triumphs, vulnerabilities and treasures, somewhere ultimately she could share her feelings about the secondary cancer which was ravaging her body.*

*But though physically weak and in pain, her spirit triumphed as she rose to the challenge of finding the way of faith. In 1988 she had joined her husband in worshipping at Holy Trinity, South Wimbledon, after he had started going to church again. She wrote down her thoughts about dying at his suggestion for the parish magazine, but they were never published in case they produced too great a wealth of visitors. They were however printed in her funeral service sheet.*

*Rosie's friends remember her for being loving and wise, a sensitive listener, with a zany sense of humour.*

17 August 1991

## Endings and Beginnings

This year I learnt that I have terminal cancer which the doctors cannot cure, but only help me to live and die more comfortably. This is hard news as I don't want to die and leave my family so young. I want to live. And yet I find myself at present amidst contradiction within myself. Where I would expect to feel panic I feel calm; where I look for frustration I find acceptance; where I might see despair I see hope; where I expect fear I find trust and peace of mind; where I might see misery I actually feel happiness. Does that perhaps sound awful to you? I must admit to feeling a little guilty that I feel – most of the time – so oddly right about life. As if it were inappropriate to feel this way. But perhaps it is that being a Christian is full of contradiction. It is through the death of Jesus that we come to God; it is through giving that we receive; by being unimportant in worldly terms that we become true children of God. So perhaps the time we begin to live life most fully can be the time we are aware of dying.

Life can certainly be viewed as a journey, and we as travellers on the road. I like to see it as an adventure with excitement, hope and fascination always just around the corner: in darker moments this hope, coupled with curiosity, has kept me running and peeping around it. And the journey for me has always been towards death and then another life. That feels the same as ever and the same for each of us. Now, however, that I know my earthly time is severely limited – although whether I have days or weeks or even months left to me I don't know – the inescapable brevity of my life feels more real – has to be believed now without any mental tricks of forgetfulness that I actually have to die. So I'm going through a series of endings with a view to a new beginning: the beginning of 'the afterlife', of 'everlasting life'. This is what Jesus has promised us, that all who know him will share in the life everlasting. That is a new beginning, and one which I can believe in and can look forward to. But what is surprising me at present is that the beginnings have already begun. This is proving to be a great and lovely gift. I am finding beginnings in relationship; with my father and siblings, with my husband and children, with my friends. Once one has dared – and it's harder for others at this time, I think, than it is for me – to talk about death and fear and pain, once the barrier has been crossed it's wonderfully liberating and can become quite relaxing, to continue to talk about these things and to admit to our mutual feelings of loss and anger and distress. It's also been a great joy for me, not only to say how much I love and need that person and appreciate them, but also the surprising fact that my relationship with them is changing now, alongside the passage of the ending . . . I am having to accept a rather premature end, but I've been given the opportunity of preparation and that is a gift.

10 September 1991

As I write we are still seeing day after day of beautiful sunshine, days which have stretched right through August into September, wonderful gifts of days. And for me this year has been special, unique, since I was told in the spring that I have incurable cancer, meaning that we have to assume that this summer has been my last one here in human life.

The beauty I see around me in nature; the love and care shown by people to others, to me; the soft, sensitive covering as if by silken shawls of God's love for each of us, that I can almost feel wrapping protectively around us; the inquisitive search for meaning and truth in our lives; the reaching out to God through Jesus; this summer has taught me so much, has opened up new understandings. And yet, of course, there is

171

enormous sadness at leaving this life so soon. I want to stay, particularly having discovered new things. And I want to stay with my family and friends. And I cannot. I have to accept this limitation. And I have doubt and fear and uncertainty. I also have reassurance and comfort and security. Emotions can run very fast, one to another.

This note is to tell you what our present position is as a family, but also to say that we haven't given up heart. We are each on our journey, of course, and the death of our human body is an appallingly painful block in the way, and one I would rather avoid. But that is not possible, and I know there will be a continued life in Christ after it; what I must do is place myself in the hand of Jesus and he will be with me along the way.

*Rosie Hopper*

# *Women and Achievement*

The traditional stereotype of the 'good Christian woman' who sits at home and spins, dies hard. In many churches today she is still she who sends out her man to fulfil his destiny with an impeccably ironed shirt, darned socks, a full belly and a peaceful soul. Edith Stein, the Jewess who became a Carmelite nun and eventually perished in Auschwitz, put it a little more bluntly. 'Man', she said, uses woman 'to achieve his own ends in the exercise of his work, and the pacifying of his lust'. But the truth is that throughout the centuries women have managed to break out of the strictures of the stereotype, to make their mark for God in their own inimitable way. One such person was Elizabeth Fry (1780–1845), the great Quaker prison reformer. She wrote:

> No person will deny the importance attached to the character and conduct of a woman, in all her domestic and social relations, when she is filling the station of a daughter, a wife, a mother, or a mistress of a family. But it is a dangerous error to suppose that the duties of females end here. Their gentleness, their natural sympathy with the afflicted, their quickness of discernment, their openness to religious impressions, are points of character (not unusually to be found in our sex) which evidently qualify them, within their own peculiar province, for a far more extensive field of usefulness.

## A Litany For Many Voices

I am Eve.
I took the apple.
Adam ate it too
but I got all the blame.

I am Sarah.
Like many a wife
I packed and followed
obedient to his call,
not mine.

I am Miriam, prophetess,
with a timbrel danced and sang.
Led the women celebrating –
Sisters, join our dance.

Samson was strong
but my guile was stronger,
I am Delilah.

I have no name but Jephthah's
daughter.
He sacrificed me to his cruel god.
O mourn with me
my lost virginity.

I am Jezebel of ill-renown,
trampled by horses, eaten by dogs,
but I painted my eyes and adorned my head
and met death wearing my crown.

I, Vashti, knew my worth,
refused to come at a royal command,
so threatening all men on earth.

I am Judith, eloquent and wise,
who did not consider my own life
but God-empowered took my knife
and hacked off Holofernes' head.

I am old and brown.
From womb to grave I have
mothered and mourned
for I am Naomi the wise.
I discerned in Ruth a love unknown.

I am Anna.
I knew what to say.
I did not keep silent in the temple.
I knew God when I saw him and said so.

I am Martha
who set the table, got the tea
and served Jesus and Mary.
It's hard to be left to work alone.

I am a woman about to be stoned.
I dared to take a lover.
I saw man-faces angry and
threatening.
Jesus the man looked in the sand
and found no condemnation.

I am woman in the crowd
who dared in faith to touch.
Such brief encounter
was my healing.

I, Mary, of Magdala,
followed to the end,
weeping stood beside the tomb
and saw, I saw the risen Lord.

I, Lydia, seller of purple,
heard good news
and shared my baptism.

I am Tabitha,
finest of needleworkers,
raised from the dead.

I am Mary.
I loved my baby
for which eternally I must wear
the patriarchal crown.
I beseech you, my sisters,
help me remove the weight
and lay it down.

*Janet Crawford and Erice Webb*

*It seems quite in keeping both with God's sense of justice, and his sense of humour, that the greatest success stories often involve the least likely people, people passed over by our plastic-money worshipping society, and, sadly, by a personality-worshipping Church! For eight years JENNIFER REES LARCOMBE had been confined to a wheelchair by repeated bouts of encephalitis. On four occasions she had nearly died. Despite her disability she had become well-known in the Church as a writer and speaker, challenging many by her fight against pain, stress and handicap.*

176

*In 1990 she was healed. God's vehicle in that story was no famous minister or preacher, but a young, black, single-parent mum called Wendy, who had known little else but sadness and rejection, until her life was changed by an encounter with Christ, just a few weeks before she went to hear Jennifer Rees Larcombe speak.*

I did not faint, and as I began to speak I actually forgot about the pain in my head. I did not do my talk well, the words and ideas came out muddled – just as they always did on a bad-pain day . . .

When the clock on the wall told me it was time to break for lunch, I said, 'Are there any comments or questions just before we close?'

Right in the very front row sat a young woman who must have been in her twenties.

'Excuse me,' she said quietly, 'but what is actually wrong with you?'

I simply said, 'Oh I've had five attacks of encephalitis', and tried to hurry on to someone else. But she went on talking and I noticed that she looked acutely embarrassed.

'I've never had anything like this happen to me before,' she mumbled, 'I've only been coming to church for a few months, you see. But I feel God is telling me to tell you that you are going to get well.'

It had happened. I do not know how I knew, but there was never any doubt in my mind that here was the person I had waited to meet for so long.

'Would you mind saying that again?' I asked. 'You see I've waited three months to hear someone tell me that.'

As she nervously repeated herself, I burst into tears of sheer relief. Jo stood up hastily and played another song while people all over the church looked as if they were wondering whatever was happening.

'She has to pray and lay hands on me', I thought. 'It was all part of the promise.' But as everyone began to surge in the direction of the refreshments I lost sight of the young woman completely. A buffet lunch was served in the basement. Obviously there was no way I was going to get down there, but food was the last thing I cared about just then. So many people wanted to be prayed for that Viv, Penny, Jo and I were all kept busy. Then as the hands of the clock crept towards half past one I began to think, 'Suppose that girl doesn't come back for the afternoon session?'

But she was there ... For three months I had been wondering what kind of person would be sent to me. 'She looks so young', I thought. 'I'll have to move very quickly at the end of this song, or I'll lose her again.' I do not remember feeling excited, I merely felt compelled to reach her before it was too late. When Viv had finally closed the meeting, I pushed back the wheels of my chair violently in the direction of the front row, with a complete disregard for intervening toes.

'Please,' I said breathlessly, 'would you mind praying for me?' She gazed at me in silent dismay, so I continued, 'I'm sure if you laid hands on me, I would be healed.'

'Didn't I make it clear,' she said looking down helplessly at me, 'all this kind of thing is new to me? I've only been a Christian for just over a year. I don't have a gift of healing. I wouldn't be able to pray for you properly.'

'Please . . .' I said urgently, but just at that moment someone came up to offer me a cup of tea. By the time I looked back the young woman was gone and I just caught sight of her disappearing out of the back door of the church. My emotions seemed to have been shooting up and down like a yo-yo for the last few days, but at that moment they reached their lowest point. Never have I wanted a cup of tea less in my life.

'She's gone!' I said.

'You mean Wendy?' said the lady with the tray of cups.

'She's probably gone home to feed her baby.'

But Wendy had not gone home. Instead she had dashed in search of one of the church leaders.

'You'll have to come and pray for this woman,' she said as she burst into his office, 'I'm just not the right kind of person to do it.'

'I'm sorry, but I can't pray for her either', he said when he had managed to help her explain. 'You have been given this conviction, so you must pray.' With that he sent her back into the church to find me.

Many people had gone home by then, but quite a crowd still lingered and they formed a circle around us.

'What do I do now?' asked Wendy diffidently. I seem to remember someone telling her to place her hands on my head and they added, 'Just allow God to use your hands as you pray, then his power can flow through them.'

She was so nervous I could feel her hands shaking and I really cannot remember the words she used except that her prayer did not contain any flowery theological phrases. She simply asked Jesus Christ to make me well.

I felt absolutely nothing. No sensations nor even any emotion. Just the matter of fact satisfaction of knowing a job had been done at long last.

When I opened my eyes no one gazed at me to see if I would stand up, because no one really expected that I would.

'Well,' I said when people began to drift away, 'I'm not going out of here in a wheelchair.' The moment I moved I knew something was different. Whenever I had been sitting upright for a time my muscles used to stiffen until they locked me rigidly into that position. Before I could attempt to stand, it used to take a very long time and a great deal of effort to get my knees and hips to straighten themselves out. That day I simply stood up.

*Jennifer Rees Larcombe*

It's always nice to know you're making some kind of impression on the world, which is why a friend of mine, a vicar's wife, was delighted when a member of the congregation came up to her after a service to tell her what an inspiration she was to the women in the church. Jo positively glowed with pleasure and tried to decide which of her many gifts and talents she had so selflessly and hitherto so thanklessly employed for the good of the church were at last bearing fruit. Was it perhaps her prayer life? Her leadership gifts? Her occasional preaching, or confidence as a woman? On the other hand it may well have been her counselling skills; the loving, pastoral care she was always at pains to provide; the patient way she dealt with the constant stream of callers and telephone calls. The possibilities seemed endless. She could hardly contain her curiosity as she waited in anticipation to discover what it was about her ministry that was so appreciated.

'In what way am I an inspiration?' she asked.

'No one,' came the enthusiastic reply, 'until you came to the church, was wearing coloured tights. You've given us all permission to go out and buy some.'

Jo was too amused to be crestfallen. Perhaps her ego needed to take a little knock. But as she thought about it later, she wondered if she ought not to feel rather affirmed all the same. Perhaps the coloured tights were a kind of symbol, a symbol of individuality, freedom and fun. Wholeness, that very hallmark of Christian life, was about having the confidence to be fully, happily oneself, and giving others the courage to be themselves too. If, inadvertently, she had said it was all right to be a little more daring, a little more colourful, a little more confident, then perhaps she had achieved more than she had ever anticipated – and not by preaching and teaching and praying. A pair of coloured tights had shown her that as far as her ministry in the church was concerned, it was not what she said but who she was that counted.

*Michele Guinness*

180

# A Woman's Brokenness

Suffering is not an experience anyone would court, but those who write about it seem to agree that the resulting brokenness is permanently destructive, wasted, only when negated or left unresolved. The potential is always there, as Jane Grayshon says, for a groan of pain to be transformed into a song of praise. Because God himself was broken for us, we are 'broken to be healed', even when, as in the case of the minister's wife whose story Joyce Huggett tells, the brokenness is of our own making. God is a master at taking the splintered fragments of our lives and painstakingly putting them back together, piece by piece. And the re-created version of our former selves can be stronger, richer, more productive, than anything that preceded it. 'Hell hath no fury like a woman scorned', said Shakespeare, and surely, of all the soul-destroying experiences women have to face, few match up to divorce. But Rae Williams tells us at the end of the section that even here, in the depths of misery and despair, fury and rejection can be transformed into something positive for those who are prepared to wait, and receive. Out of apparent death springs new life: 'Unless a seed fall into the ground and die, it remains a single grain, but if it does die it produces many grains.'

## Broken

Broken
by the wheel of the car
driving me to the next
appointment

Broken
by the tearing tensions
of demanding opposing
compartments of my life

Broken
by the fall
from the pedestal
on which I chose to stand

Broken
by disappointment
of those who thought me
strong and sure

Broken
by impermeable silence
unseen waves of mute resistance
from life denying loss

Broken by words of bitterness
and hatred
spewed from a dark
and unimagined
place within

Broken
by angry taunts
of those who would not hear
my fear full words

Broken
the glass-like
clarity of vision
into a thousand jagged frosty fragments
splintering the ground

Broken
steadfastly
as bread is broken
broken to be shared
among us

Broken
to be healed

*Jean Clark*

## Do Not Kiss Me

Do not kiss me now
Do not come too close
It's every breath which I must breathe
Now
and again now . . .

    I hear a groan with each one
    Is that my voice?
    I do not mean to grunt.

If I hold my breath
Does that help?
. . . I cannot.
My body's past such pride.
Instead I'll delay each one . . .

Just stroke me now
My arm,
My forehead,
Run your fingers through my hair.
Without words,
Sooth me
Reach me
in this world with no words
this world where tears will not flow
for anguish.

Ah! Staccato stabbing
Pain piercing
Throbbing
Punctuated by these cries
Suppressed
But not silenced.

Would that this were singing
and not a cry of distress!
Oh my God; my God! . . .

Accept each groan
each involuntary groan
and make it into
a song for You.

*Jane Grayshon*

Peter had often commented that trouble sends us no telegraphed warnings. So we discovered. Three years after Peter John's birth, I was to find out that even our greatest human desire and all out effort are never enough.

Suddenly illness struck me down. Having almost fainted at a church meeting, I went to John Hopkins' in Baltimore for a complete physical check-up.

After days of tests and X-rays, Dr Thomas Sprunt's summary of my medical situation was devastating. The diagnosis was tuberculosis, with me ordered to bed full time. 'Since tests have uncovered no infection-spreading bacilli,' the doctor explained, 'you can stay at home. But you should not, must not, do any housework or, in fact, work of any kind.'

'But – but I can't go to bed,' I stammered out. 'I have a three-year-old son. He needs me.'

'Mrs Marshall,' the voice was stern, 'total bed rest is mandatory. You have no choice. There is no other cure. Just consider yourself fortunate that it's not a sanatorium.'

'Then how long do you think it will take me to get well?' My voice was now almost a whisper.

Dr Sprunt hesitated a long moment. 'Oh, possibly three or four months.' Then seeing my stricken face, 'Mrs Marshall, please don't feel so badly about it. People do recover from tuberculosis.'

When I later rushed sobbing into Peter's arms to blurt out the news, he was as stunned as I. For once, this most articulate of men was without words and mutely tried to comfort me with touches and caresses.

Dr Sprunt turned my case over to a Washington lung specialist. A trained nurse was necessary because I was not even allowed to feed myself. Any arm motion might interfere with healing of the chest. Miss Mildred Beall, an RN from our church, volunteered for the emergency.

The specialist's orders: between-meal eggnogs to put weight on me; temperature to be taken six times a day and recorded;

one chest X-ray per month; I could get out of bed only to go to the nearby bathroom.

But who would take care of Peter John? And how would any of us explain what was happening to a desolate three-year-old who needed his mother?

Our son was given a tuberculin skin test. Results: negative. So he was allowed to trot in and out of the bedroom. Years later, an indelible picture rises to meet me . . . Peter John, tall for his age at three, standing with his back to one of the windows, the light behind him making an aureole of his blonde curls, staring at me lying there flat in bed, his big round blue eyes sad, hurt, and questioning.

It took all the will-power I had to keep from jumping out of bed and running to him to hug him close.

There was no way. There stood the nurse watchfully, with sympathetic eyes.

'You can sit on the bed, and I'll tell you a story', I told Peter John limply. 'Maybe later on we can play games together.'

Sorry substitutes. I knew full well that such makeshift gestures could not provide the security our son needed. My mother came to take care of him and stayed as long as she could. There followed a long string of maids, nursemaids and assorted government girls. Help of any kind was very scarce, for we were now two years into World War II.

And so one interminable month dragged by after another.

On an especially low day Peter would often stand in the bedroom looking down at me propped up on the pillows, and turn prophet. 'Cath'rine, someday you will look back with gratitude on these bleak days as some of the richest in your life.' Then, seeing my incredulous inability to receive his words: 'Besides, Cath'rine, you know perfectly well, all discouragement is from Satan.'

I just wanted to throw a book at my Scottish prophet. Whereupon he would grin and pat my cheek and kiss me, turn on his heel and depart for the church office.

186

Yet looking back, I know that Peter was right. For me those two years in bed were a continuation in depth of the voyage of self-discovery and God-discovery begun in college.

*Catherine Marshall*

A friend of mine explained to me how God had met her in the depths of despair through a vision.

She was married to a pastor but had indulged in an affair with a married man. Eventually, the realization dawned that she had reached a crossroads. Either she must leave her husband and children and cause untold hurt to numerous people, or she must give up her lover. She chose the latter.

Having repented of the illicit love-affair, she wandered into the woods to think and to pray. As she continued to pour out the bitterness of her soul to God, she described her life to him as nothing more than fragments of her former self. While she stood, silent and still before God, into her mind came a picture of the fragments she had described: they littered the ground like so many pieces of red clay. As she gazed at the broken vessel representing her life, into the picture came Jesus. She saw the tenderness of his face and observed the sensitivity of his fingers as he stooped down and started to turn over those forlorn fragments. 'Suddenly, he started to piece them together', she told me. 'He assured me that, though the vessel was a mess, every tiny piece of the pot was precious. I watched the skill with which he put the pieces together again. He re-created that vessel. He showed me that it would be even more useful. Then he glazed it and held it up for me to see. I couldn't see a single sign of the joins where the cracked parts had been pressed back together.'

For that woman, this vision came to her as a promise from

God which guaranteed her future with him. It also com-
municated the much-needed message of healing and forgiveness
which motivated her to walk away from the sin of the past and
to work at her marriage again.

*Joyce Huggett*

'*Every day,*' *says KATHY KEAY,* '*thousands of Single Profes-
sionals come home from the World of Work, many to an empty
house. There's no one to scream at, apart from the cat.*'
    *This piece of writing vividly catches the potentially hollow
existence of the thousands who are alone in a society where a
relationship is the norm. But it also looks beyond the gaping
void to a new appreciation of some of the good things, often
taken for granted by those who have no obvious need of them,
which can help to fill it, a little.*

## In Solidarity

I know what it's like
to want to break out
from the bounds of
established morality

To want to love,
the temptation of adultery.
I know the frustrations
of poverty
the confines of having
One room,

188

Restricted space
Stifled creativity.
I know too, the dehumanizing effects
of having no job,
of being outside
the rhythm of the working world.
Day after day
Left with yourself
thrown continually
upon your own resources
tortured by memories of
Past usefulness

I know the crippling effects
of Wounds re-opened
in relationships.
Powerlessness
in the face of Death
The misunderstanding of friends,
Never knowing where the next meal's coming from,
with whom you will eat it
or when.

Yet amidst all of Life's Prescribed Afflictions
there remains:
the reality of Unbroken Friendship
the beauty of music and flowers
the companionship of books
the joy of colours
and of Redefining yourself
in Clothes.
Laughter and Spontaneity,

Unexpected encouragements
through letters and phone calls
And You my God
In Me
Restoring Life's Beauty
in brokenness

*Kathy Keay*

*The end of a marriage brings its own very particular sense of aloneness, for it is a compulsory state imposed unexpectedly and often unwillingly, compounded by feelings of rejection and failure.*

*RAE WILLIAMS, who is a teacher and mother of two boys, was married for nineteen years, fifteen of them to a minister of the Church. When her marriage came to an end she had to leave home suddenly, with no goodbyes. Nothing prepared her for the searing pain and crushing sense of loss that divorce can bring.*

*The situation of the divorced person in the Church is ambiguous, she claims. 'We may have children, but do not fit the typical family model. We have been bereaved, but it is not acknowledged. Bereavement is kosher. Divorce is not. It shouldn't happen. It disturbs our tidy view of the world.'*

*But for Rae the most disturbing aspect of divorce is the fear that since a person has rejected you, God may have abandoned you too. In this meditation she explores that wintry feeling of abandonment and the slow realization that even in winter the seeds of spring lie buried in the soil.*

## New Life in the Hidden Place

Hidden in the ground
the seed lies sleeping,
Softly the autumn leaves fall,
Bare twigs against a stark sky.
My God, where are you?

Silence.

Why aren't you there when I need you most?
I rage against heaven, then lie weary
Exhausted by the struggle,

Alone.

Deep in the dark
the bulb lies hidden
Nothing stirring.
All is still.
My God, where are you?

Silence.

'Why don't you do something?'
I sit in sadness
Remembering the good times.

Alone.

There is a time for waiting,
a time for growing,
When the tomb becomes a womb,
a place of growth,

New life springs up,
Slowly, tentatively,
Roots reach down,
New shoots uncurl.

'My child reach out,
Accept new life,
Feel my embrace,
Receive my tears,
Shed for you.
In your rage
I was there.
In your sadness
I was there.

Yet you turned away,
You beat your fists against me
And could not receive my love.
You could not bear the brightness of my face.
When you felt so alone,
In the cold
In the dark,
And said I wasn't there,
I was holding you,
pressed up against me so close,
you could not see my face.'

*Rae Williams*

# Friendship

'How wonderful was your love for me, better even than the love of women', says King David of his friendship with Jonathan. Few men in our present society discover and enjoy that kind of intimacy in their relationships. And what they miss!

The novelist George Eliot captured the essence of real friendship when she wrote, 'Friendship is the inexpressible comfort of feeling safe with a person; having neither to weigh up thoughts, nor measure words.'

Women often do find that kind of delightful rapport with each other, that ability to relax completely in the other's company. Occasionally they find it with men. But they have much less to lose than men. There is less 'weighing up' and 'measuring', for they tend to be less competitive, more in touch with their emotions, more accepting of the other, more used to pooling shared experience and giving of themselves.

Occasionally men are able to understand and value that, enjoying for themselves the quality and quantity of friendship women give, responding in kind. And when they do, a new and special kind of relationship is born.

*It seems fitting to begin this section where the last ended, with Rae Williams, for friendship can be a God-given way of bringing healing to the broken-hearted. If only, as George Eliot says, words are not allowed to get in the way.*

The Church is good with words:
    smooth words
    comforting words
    impressive words
    glorious words
    moving words
Words roll off the tongue.
Words make things manageable, controllable, tidy.

What can we say in the face of the inexpressible?
    I don't know what to say
    I feel tongue-tied
    I was going to write
    I've been thinking of you
    I meant to drop you a line
    How can I say that I care?

    Give me a HUG
    'I care' without words
    When I'm suffering
    I don't need words
I just need to know you are there
That someone would notice if I disappeared
    And if I matter to you
    And I matter to God
then life is worth living.

*Rae Williams*

*Here is another relationship which found words extraneous and unnecessary. Yet no one can deny the quality of contact. For it left ANN MORRISH with her most vivid and enriching memory of a holiday in Greece. Perhaps it is not without significance that Ann is a member of the Quakers and says that silence is very important to her.*

*She trained as an actress at the Old Vic Theatre School and has since worked extensively in the theatre, television and radio in this country and Canada. But Wales appears to have all but supplanted the stage in her heart, for she now combines acting with farming in the Brecon Beacons, writes poetry and gives 'Special Hours' to children.*

I looked up and saw her
Watching me
Sitting as I was
In the shade of an olive tree
On the other side of the fence.
It was the hottest part of the afternoon
No breeze at all
Just baking stillness
A woman of my own age
Grey-haired but strong still
In a faded blue dress
Brown hard-working hands with broken nails
And in her lap
An old straw hat,
Her face in shadow
Grey eyes calmly watching me.
Like reflections in still water
We looked at one another
The only sound
The ceaseless scratching of cicadas
A gentle exhalation rippled the reflections
And overhead the branches rustled slightly
I looked up and saw
Small green olives
Forming among the leaves

And the shifting patterns of light and shadow.
When I looked back
She'd gone.
Later between the rows of olive trees
I saw a peasant woman in an old straw hat
Breaking the hard soil
With a mattock.

*Ann Morrish*

*In separation, only words will suffice. But many say that a deeper, truer friendship can be born out of letter-writing than out of personal contact, for we can pour out on paper thoughts and feelings we might not be able to say to someone's face. The telephone, isolating the relationship from both heart-to-heart and eyeball-to-eyeball contact, has a great deal to answer for.*

Dear Hannah

Time tested friend
how I thank God for you
as I pour out
my soul through Paper celebrations
Paper Prayers
written and received
across many miles
Necessary Miracles
of Communication.
You, like God
and so many of my
Loved Ones,

are Far Away
on earth
in heaven –
Yet you are
more Real to me
than many who are Near
and more part of my life
than people
whom I can see or touch.
As iron sharpens iron,
So your life
committed to the abolition of apartheid
helps keep
the Cutting Edge
in mine.

No Woman is an Island
and no continents can separate
people of like mind.

*Kathy Keay*

*Friendship sustains many women in the most difficult situations, not only in the pain of loss faced by Rae Williams, or in the intense loneliness of singleness as experienced by Kathy Keay, but also when we are 'up against it all', finding ourselves face to face with 'the system'. It is then that we discover how the sisterhood of women, and the support of many men, can feed us.*

*As a pastoral assistant in the Roman Catholic Church, SISTER ELIZABETH REES has worked in a variety of parishes for the last fifteen years. Now on the staff of Hawkstone Hall*

*Pastoral Centre, near Shrewsbury, giving workshops to all who come for renewal, she loves her job of nurturing, but it is not easy. 'Being a woman in the Church is rather like being a woodworm, gnawing away at the planks of an ancient institution until all that is outmoded crumbles away, and the song of thousands of joyful woodworms reaches the stars.'*

*But she is in no doubt about what keeps her gnawing!*


What have been the joys of my work these last fifteen years? First, I know the joy of fulfilment, of setting out on an adventure to which I felt called by God, and on which I have been nurtured by the Spirit at each point along the way. Someone has to be a pioneer, and I am proud that I have been invited by God to be one.

Next, I know the joy of watching a community grow in faith and confidence, as I feed it with God's life. Since I have been pushed around fairly often, I have been able to nurture a variety of different communities – more than I myself would have chosen. Then there has been the joy of working in collaboration with some of the finest priests in the country, feeling trusted and valued by them.

Finally, I have become a woman of the Church. I have seen through the rotting structures – they have mostly dealt death to me – and I have discovered God in the hearts of men and women who are the living stones of the Church. I have formed deep friendships with men and women who have loved me, counselled me, inspired me and suffered with me. I now feel firmly part of the Body of Christ, and I know the sap that flows through the vine from branch to branch, from me to you, and from you to me. I know the sap because it sustains me. It is called love.

*Sister Elizabeth Rees*

*Matthew Hallam began writing creatively when he was in the sixth form at Nottingham High School, where he won the poetry prize, but has been particularly inspired in recent years by several, very special, life-enhancing relationships, particularly with women, which have brought him a measure of friendship he hadn't believed possible.*

*Born in Mansfield in 1970, after several years of social work he is now teaching English in Eastern Europe. He plans to read for a degree in psychology.*

### Gift for Patricia

Walk with me
a little way

Lift me up
if you please

Knock me down
and we shall sing

Place me in your pocket
spread me around

Open my mind
discover my heart

Hear my voice
if you like its sound

Dance with me
and we shall sing

Laugh with me
for we have cried

I am your friend
I'm by your side.

*Matthew Hallam*

# Women's Spirituality

When women explore the more mystical aspect of their faith 'dog-tiredness' seems to be a prevailing factor: the dog-tiredness of the mother, like Angela Ashwin, with children at her elbow and dirty dishes in the sink; the dog-tiredness of the single woman, like Sheila Cassidy, giving her all for her job or ministry, with no one to say, 'Stop! That's enough for today'; the dog-tiredness of the carer, like Anne Townsend, who cannot find anyone to listen to her inner cry for support. But each of these women, though they may have come to the very end of their inner resources, has discovered, like wise old Mother Maribel of Wantage, that even that oh-so-human dog-tiredness can be offered up to God.

More than that, no matter what our calling in life, reserving space for leisure, recreation and self-discovery is in itself a right and spiritual thing to do, since God does not 'use' us to keep the world turning for him. Rather he prefers a companion, who will sometimes watch, enjoy and admire what he does. We are invited to make him our first love, not to work until we drop.

Small wonder that children, with their spontaneity, sense of fun and play, have so much to teach adults about the spiritual life. Theirs is the simplicity, trust, freedom and abandoned joy we need to discover and emulate. For, as some of the writers here have discovered, God invites us to be his partner in the dance, even if the steps are hard to learn.

*MOTHER MARIBEL of Wantage (1887–1970) trained at the Slade as an artist before she became a religious at the Community of St Mary the Virgin in Wantage, Oxfordshire. Her 'stations of the cross'. carved in teak, can be seen at the convent today.*

Dog-tiredness is such a lovely prayer, really, if only we would recognize it as such. Sometimes I hear, 'I'm so dog-tired when I get to chapel, I can't pray'. But what does it matter? We don't matter. Our Lord can pray just as well through a dog-tired body and mind as through a well-rested one, better perhaps. It is the same with pain and suffering of all kinds. Our advance guard on the Infirmary Wing would tell us that.

*Mother Maribel CSMV*

I think I can draw two major truths from my own experience of depression, exhaustion, burnout, whatever it should be called. The first is the lesson of humility . . . I do not have the strength to do all the things I want to do . . . I need time to myself, I need to pray, to play, to read, to be with friends, to have fun . . . Do we not owe it to those we serve to accept our limitations and cherish our minds and bodies so that we will be available to serve them a little longer? I have learned to be very wary of the famous prayer of St Ignatius, 'to give and not to count the cost'.

*Sheila Cassidy*

*DR ANNE TOWNSEND was a missionary for many years with the Overseas Missionary Fellowship in Thailand. Her medical background, her many books, and later her role as the founder*

202

*of* Family *magazine, made her an authority in the evangelical wing of the Church on a wide range of issues to do with relationships and spirituality. As a woman she achieved an unprecedented acknowledgement of her gifts when she was invited to become director of the Care Trust (Christian Action, Research and Education), an organization committed to promoting Christian standards and family life in an increasingly secular society.*

*Then one day, feeling like an 'unlovable, fat, ugly stinking female rat scurrying with increasing desperation round and round an endless treadmill . . . overwhelmed by the explosive build-up of pressure within me', she attempted to take her own life. The stress of a job which demanded answers she could not give and responses she was too tired to make, combined with living up to the 'platform and pulpit' image of a successful church leader, running a home and never having the opportunity to deal with a vast backlog of unresolved grief and pain, all proved too much.*

*The attempt failed, and there ensued a long and painful struggle to a reality she had never known before, to the discovery of a new self, to new beginnings. She is now a deacon in the Church of England and works part time as a chaplain in a London teaching hospital.*

This year I have had a summer to beat all summers. I don't know what possessed me and made me buy walking shoes for the first time in my life, jeans in which I could bend and books of local walks. Something urged me out to explore places of which I had never heard before. I joined the National Trust and the Royal Horticultural Society. You know that in the past I would have thought it was a waste of money to support organizations like those. I even used to think that it was a waste of time to be going out and exploring like this – 'every second must be made to count for God' – and that meant non-stop working or engaging in 'obviously' Christian activities.

So this summer I have wonderful, totally new memories of long sunny days. Who cares if the rest of Britain thought it rained more than usual – it didn't rain once in my world! I have memories, new to me as an adult, of lying in the sun on the lawns of Ham House, sparrows pecking my arms and grey squirrels pinching my cake, smelling lavender and hearing the faint buzz of bees in a distant garden. I have memories of sitting on the river bank at Ham, day-dreaming for hours, until you disturbed me. There were the unexpected twinges of your presence as I wandered under the trees and round the ponds in Richmond Park. I found time to stand and gaze up at giant trees at Wisley and to sense the vast limitlessness of eternity. I sat sun-soaked, warm in your love, by the canal at Wisley watching barges negotiate the lock. I delighted in the wind whipping my hair on the cliffs at Barton-on-Sea, depositing its salty calling card on my lips. I caught the boom of bitterns in the estuary of Hordle beach, and marvelled at the dappled beauty of deer in the New Forest.

My friend said that I sounded just like a seven-year-old when we went blackberry picking. But, God, I do feel just about that age! For too long I have felt prematurely old, as if the weight of the world was mine, but no more! My heart has skipped and danced, and felt like a kite released to swing in huge arcs where it will cross the sky.

*Anne Townsend*

*DOROTHY DAY (1897–1980) was a Roman Catholic laywoman who founded the Catholic Worker Movement, and worked tirelessly for peace and human rights.*

When a mother, a housewife, asks what she can do, one can only point to the way of St Thérèse, that little way, so much understood and so much despised. She did all for the love of God, even to putting up with the irritation in herself caused by the proximity of a nervous nun. She began with working for peace in her own heart, and willing to love where love was difficult, and so she grew in love, and increased the sum total of love in the world, not to speak of peace.

Paper work, cleaning the house, cooking the meals, dealing with innumerable visitors who come all through the day, answering the phone, keeping patience and acting intelligently, which is to find some meaning in all these encounters – these things too are the work of peace, and often seem like a very little way.

*Dorothy Day*

*CARYLL HOUSELANDER (1901–54) was a Roman Catholic laywoman, a prolific writer of poetry and prose. While she was still a teenager she had several profound mystical experiences which formed the foundation for much of her writing.*

We all know the woman who is exaggeratedly house-proud, who concentrates on the neatness, cleanliness, beauty of her house, to the exclusion of its comfort. Her house is not a home, nothing must ever be left about, out of place. To come in with muddy shoes is a crime; it is a crime to disarrange the cushions! In such a house one can neither work nor rest, one is never at home, because it is not a home.

There are many women who are 'soul-proud' in the same way. They spend their whole time cleaning up their soul, turning out the rubbish, dusting and polishing. Like the house-proud woman they become nervous, tired; there is nothing left in them to give, they have wasted themselves on the silver, the curtains, the ornaments.

Christ wants to be at home in your soul. He will not go away and leave you if the house is chilly and uncomfortable; he loves you too much to leave you, but how often, how tragically often he must say nowadays: 'The Son of Man has nowhere to lay his head.'

Christ asks for a home in your soul, where he can be at rest with you, where he can talk easily to you, where you and he, alone and together, can laugh and be silent and be delighted with one another.

All this may seem daring, but it is true, it is the meaning of the incarnation.

*Caryll Houselander*

It is surprising how tempting it is to ignore the opportunity to pray when it does arise. In the mornings I often have a chance to be alone with God while the children are at school. But the breakfast dishes need washing up, and then I must hoover downstairs, put the washing machine on and go shopping. It is a real struggle to let go of all this for a moment and sit down and pray, while I'm looking at the cornflakes stuck to the sides of the cereal bowls. I am pulled in two directions. I long to have a space to pray, but I also long to leap up and wash the dishes. If I do succumb to the lure of the kitchen (which is never strong at other times) it is fatal. As soon as I've finished washing the last spoon, you can guarantee that the doorbell will ring and my chance for a quiet time with God will be lost altogether.

It is so easy to be like the men in the parable and make excuses to miss the banquet.

*Angela Ashwin*

*Since, traditionally, women have given children the time and opportunity to give away their spiritual gems, it has been women, rather than men, who have been most challenged and enriched by them. And it doesn't always have anything to do with whether we are mothers or not. Whether by nature or nurture, we appear to have a heightened awareness of the special nuances children bring into their relationships and conversations.*

*For CLARE RICHARDS, whose children were adopted, as for Catherine Booth Clibborn ('La Marechale', William and Catherine Booth's eldest daughter, who founded the work of the Salvation Army in France), children are closer to God than adults, for their spiritual sensitivities have not been diluted by adult sophistication.*

There are times when Pedro shows a greater wisdom than mine. He did just this when he was three years old and I watched him, unseen, at playgroup. There was a highly disturbed boy in the group. His behaviour was destructive and negative. I had secretly hoped Pedro would keep away from him and play with the conforming children. I watched the boy playing, as usual, alone in the sand pit. Suddenly Pedro approached him, slowly. He sat near him; he moved closer; he offered him a toy truck. I watched with baited breath as the boy snatched it away. Pedro stayed there quietly and within five minutes the two of them were playing peacefully together.

It is experiences like these that have made me realize the presence of God in my ordinary, everyday life. All religious words seem unnecessary in the presence of a human experience that is illuminated by love, acceptance, forgiveness and welcome.

*Clare Richards*

*While she was still a girl, CATHERINE BOOTH CLIBBORN set off to France to pioneer the work of the Salvation Army there, risking her own safety as she preached in some of the most disreputable quarters of the city. But not for nothing did she gain the nickname 'La Marechale' for she proved herself fearless, nerveless and invincible.*

*Somehow, while she continued to lead the work, with a diary bulging with preaching engagements and counselling sessions, she managed to raise five daughters and five sons, all of whom grew up to follow her into pioneering work within the Army. Her philosophy of child-rearing was never treat a child as a child; always see them as full, ministering members of the Christian community. For they in fact have spiritual insights we lack, and therefore much to teach us.*

When my third son, William Emmanuel was a child, he always had the most singular idea that Jesus was a woman. One evening he was praying, 'O Jesus, Thou art the best of all ladies in Thy heavens.' Augustine, a year older, who was kneeling by his side, corrected him . . . 'I tell you Jesus was not a lady, he was a gentleman.' Willie answered his brother slowly and thoughtfully, 'Perhaps later on he changed.' A lady from Finland was sitting in the room when this dialogue took place. She had been converted from the religion of Theosophy to Christianity through reading one of my French books. Like myself, she was deeply interested in children. Calling Willie to her side, she asked, 'Willie, why do you always think Jesus was a lady?' His answer came like a flash, 'Parce-qu'il fut si tendre envers nous' (Because he was so tender towards us). So to the mind of this child of seven, on which no school of thought had ever written, the chief characteristic of the saviour was his tenderness, and he could not reconcile this so well with a man as he could with a woman.

I wrote an article, which was translated into three languages, on this child's answer. How many of us come out of our seminaries and universities with all else but that infinite tenderness!

*Catherine Booth Clibborn*

## Praying In Extremis

Prayer is primarily giving ourselves to God, not getting what we want out of him. Nevertheless, there is an element of asking in our intercession. It is natural to ask and even beg God to help when someone is in need. At one time I scorned this idea, thinking that intercession was *only* an offering of concern. Then my three-month-old son became desperately ill. I found myself kneeling and praying with my whole heart, 'Lord, if I have ever prayed, I pray now. *Please* don't let him die.'

Looking back at that prayer of mine, I can honestly say that it was not an attempt to twist God's arm. I never felt that he was a reluctant deity needing to be cajoled into co-operating. I was pouring out my anguish and fear to God *as my Father*, almost pouring out my whole self for Andrew. I wanted God to be close, to flood the situation with his power and love.

209

Andrew did recover. We were told afterwards that we were very lucky to have him. I do not understand why my child was healed while others are not. Suffering and death are mysteries beyond our comprehension. But of one thing I am certain. One morning while sitting with Andrew, whose body was a mass of tubes and wires linked to machines, I suddenly knew that he was in God's hands, whatever should happen. I realized that he was loved and held by God, whether he recovered from this illness or not. That was what mattered, more than anything else.

This moment of heightened awareness lasted for only a short time. I soon became distraught again, worrying about Andrew's operation and chances of survival. But that flash of insight was part of my praying, and part of the intercession which lots of people were offering for him. The faith that had come from praying did not take away the nagging pain that I might lose him; but it took away the hopelessness.

*Angela Ashwin*

## Strangers on a Train

A few months ago I caught the 4.50 home from London in the nick of time. Ploughing my way through a packed train I suddenly felt decidedly hungry, and remembered that large, luscious banana which had appeared on my breakfast tray in the hotel that morning. I'd wrapped it up and saved it for just this occasion.

Eventually I found a spare seat tucked away next to a window and not wanting to disturb the passenger on the corridor side too often, decided to root for my banana and can of drink before I disposed of my bag under the seat and sat down.

It had been a very hot day. Only when my hand touched the mound of slushy mush at the bottom of my bag did I realize that my poor banana had failed to survive. My fellow-traveller stood up to let me past, then promptly sat down again when she saw my hand. I beat a hasty retreat to the toilets.

Five minutes later I returned and after a prolonged rooting session in my bag finally found my can of drink, disturbed my fellow-passenger again and took my seat. There's a knack to opening a metal can. I haven't got it! I tugged and tugged on the metal loop, which finally gave way in a great jerk, spraying orange juice all over the private papers of the gentleman across the table. 'I'm sorry', I said, and proceeded to mop him up with a tissue from my handbag. It was covered with blood. Whose? Mine! I steeled myself to look down at his papers once again and saw drops of blood all over his once pristine sheets.

'I'm sorry', I said again, wrapping up my finger and mopping his papers once more.

He muttered some vague acceptance of my apology. The companion on my left looked away in a hurry. The traveller opposite her buried himself in a book as if he had seen nothing.

I suddenly had a terrible urge to laugh. But my companions sat like expressionless dummies. No twitch of the lips. No smile of understanding, sympathy or acceptance. No acknowledgement of the mutual embarrassment shared by all human beings. We travelled together for more than two hours and never met.

'Love your neighbour as yourself', Jesus said. 'And who is my neighbour?' they asked him, obviously finding the idea as uncomfortable as we do today. And he told a story about someone who was prepared to let down the barriers and reach out to another.

*Michele Guinness*

*God the Father has an extraordinary capacity to turn misery into laughter, despair into hope, mourning into rejoicing, and potential tragedy into the deepest form of joy. JUDITH PINHEY's son Nicholas was gravely ill for seven and a half years with ME. For nearly three of those years he was almost unable to move, unable even to open his eyes. He did not speak for months on end. It was during this time of immense distress that she felt God communicating with her. The words, she said, 'are formed in my heart in silent prayer'.*

*God seemed to speak to her about 'the dance', the new life in which he holds and refreshes us. 'We are often out of step and do not want to go where he is leading, but this dance is his grace in us. We dance alone with him as we look inward, and in company with his whole creation as he turns us to look outward.'*

## The Maypole

Come and rejoice with me.

You are like dancers around a maypole, skipping and interweaving, each holding a bright ribbon attached to the top of the pole.

It is a May Day celebration. God has come to the rescue and new life is springing up. It is a day of sunshine and in the warmth of the air is the promise of summer fruitfulness.

Come, throw off the darkness of winter and the days of drudgery when your hearts were sad and weary.
This is a joyful day when each dancer knows the right steps and the pattern of the dance depends on the steadfastness of the pole.

I am the maypole, colourful and decked with flowers. I am the fixed point of your dance, the centre of your activity. I hold the strands by which you weave your lives together.

Look up and dance for the joy of the life I give. You dance in a circle of love, everlasting and large as the universe – too large for you to see the ribbons wonderfully woven, but you can see the hand that holds them and you can rejoice in such love.

*Judith Pinhey*


## God Ran Away

God ran away
when we imprisoned her
and put her in a box
named church.
God would have none
of our labels and
our limitations
and she said,
'I will escape and plant myself
in simpler soil
where those who see, will see,
and those who hear, will hear.
I will become a God – believable,
because I am free,
and go where I will.
My goodness will be found
in my freedom and
that freedom I offer to all –
regardless of colour, sex, or status,
regardless of power or money.

213

Ah, I am God
because I am free
and all those who would be free
who will find me,
roaming, wandering, singing.
Come, walk with me –
come, dance with me!
I created you to sing – to dance,
to love . . .'

If you cannot sing,
nor dance, nor love,
because they put you
also in a box,
know that your God broke free
and ran away.
So send your spirit
then, to dance with her.
Dance, sing with the God
whom they cannot tame nor chain.
Dance within, though they chain
your very guts
to the great stone walls . . .
Dance, beloved,
Ah, Dance!

*Edwina Gateley*

# Saying Goodbye and Grieving

Anger, despair, loneliness, disorientation, all form part of the grieving process. But, 'I must grow', says Anita Thorne. Whether we lose a father, husband or child, or even a treasured part of our anatomy, there is no way of skirting the pain. We must go and grow through it, or remain forever stuck, like something formed in a plaster caste, in an attitude of profound and bitter resentment.

Gradually, all those whose writings I have included here discover the bitter–sweet peace of resolution. It may come as a sense of letting go, as the sudden urge to laugh and have fun again, or as the desire to have another child. The sense of loss may never go away, but it becomes a part of the bereaved, and, in the gentle hands of God, can be turned from its potentially destructive power into a resource.

*Around 25,000 women a year discover they have breast cancer. For many this may mean radical surgery, a form of amputation, and the necessity of coming to terms with a new body. Simply knowing that the operation may save their lives is not enough, whatever the medical profession may suggest! Grieving for what has been lost is a vital part of the journey to self-acceptance and wholeness.*

*PATRICIA ABSALOM was orphaned at the age of twelve, left school at fifteen, and cared for a guardian and a granny until their death. She became a mature student at 43, suffered from depression at 52, and fought through to discover she had cancer at 59. Throughout her life sparks of excitement and joy have sustained her, and she writes, when she must, 'to make sense of everyday life'.*

## Letting Go

I miss you most of the time
less than I used to

The first time
I had folded my arms
across my chest for comfort

My right hand was filled
my left hand fell flat
against the soreness of my scar

I wept for your round fullness,
smooth, soft-honey or blue-white
skin, never particularly noticed
except when you responded to another's caress

And I'll weep for you

*Patricia Absalom*

*ANITA THORNE is a woman deacon working in a parish in Bristol. She has two grown-up daughters. She wrote this poem after the death of her father.*

216

## Grief Thoughts – Gone

The face in the bed is so white.
He is gone.
Suffered so much and so long
now gone.
The stunning truth hits,
. . . gone.

The funeral dream passes before
until the crematorium door,
nightmare breaks in.
Gone
those hands, those eyes, that smile.
Gone from me.

No do not take him away.
No please,
the heart stands still,
even though he was so ill
that is the body of one much loved.

People and noises dim in pain
the dream is in the car again
Stop the car is the silent scream.
Please don't leave this place
I must see his face
once more.

Jesus I carried him to you.
I asked you to take him out of his pain.
I must grow,
but you must know
I miss him so.

*Anita Thorne*

## Losing a Mother

Peace be to your beautified and pious soul, beloved and affectionate Mother, who gave me birth, reared me, loved, fostered and cherished me, who endured much for me all the days of your life.

You, whose maternal care was unceasingly devoted to my happiness, whose maternal eye watched over my physical and mental development, you have gone from me and nowhere can I find a guide and counsellor like you. So I took fresh strength from God, and came here, to the chamber of the one who bore me, to be with your earthly remains, wrapt in the sleep of death, while your soul has soared heavenward, and I say, peace be unto your soul, you blessed among women. May it be that for you the promise comes true, 'Arise, shine, for your light is come and the glory of the Lord is risen upon you.'

And as for me, your daughter, may I be counted worthy to see my children and children's children devoted to the Law of God, keeping the commandments, walking in the paths of righteousness while you rest in calm and quietness in the Garden of Eden, in the company of all the pious and righteous Mothers of Israel. May you, and I, be deemed worthy to rise to eternal life in fellowship with these virtuous and godly daughters at the end of time. Amen.

*Traditional Jewish prayer*

*Prolific poet, theatre critic, and playwright for stage, television and radio, MICHELENE WANDOR struggles with the Jewish faith in which she was raised. Almost despite herself, she finds that at times of crisis its thinking is woven into the fabric of her life.*

My children and I joke sporadically; Mother is in heaven with Buddy Holly, Elvis and Janis Joplin, cooking them chicken soup. If anyone needs it, they do. She is busy looking after the Messiah, so that when he (of course it's a he) decides to come down he will have all his clean clothes ready. A woman's work is never done. Anyone who dies will be welcomed by my mother's shortbread biscuits, made only with butter. Heaven in this scenario is teeming with hip folk; it is a carefully screened, cultural mecca. No pious angels, but a world in our own desired image, in which we have created our own Mother of Israel. On reflection, I'm not sure I would not be better off believing in God. But when my mother died, I found that I was glad that some people do.

*Michelene Wandor*

*BARBARA ASPELL was born on the island of Rugen off the east coast of Germany shortly before the Second World War. She and her parents were forced to flee from the advancing Soviet Communists who drove them out of their beloved island home. For weeks they marched on across a shattered Germany, pursued by the threat of starvation or execution, until they managed to reach the relative safety of West Berlin and the Allies. Barbara remembers those days vividly. She remembers lying in a forest gazing up at the stars, knowing that there was a God watching over her, who had a special plan for her life.*

*She came to England in the late sixties as an au pair, and knew, the moment she met him, that she would marry Colin Aspell. He was a clergyman, and though there were one or two difficult parishes, she loved her role as the traditional, supportive clergy wife. When he died of cancer of the bowel while still in his forties, she lost not only a husband and the father of her two girls, but her role in life and her home.*

219

*Rebuilding a new life has been a long and painful process. But she is now personal assistant to the Advisor in Multi-Cultural Relations in the Coventry Diocese, and is based at Coventry Cathedral. It is a job she has made very much her own.*

### 'till Death do us Part

Lord, you have ordained marriage as the foundation of
    life on earth.
How blessed are they that marry and grow in love to each
    other.

A glimpse of heaven Lord
to feel completely loved
to know my folly and mistakes will be forgiven
to feel secure and protected
to feel valued and appreciated.

'till death do us part.

*Why then Lord is life so fragile?*

Why Lord can life be cut off and wiped out?
Why are there accidents?
Why is there terminal illness?

You who hung on the cross
have you forgotten pain?

You who walked in the Garden of Gethsemane
have you forgotten the desolation?

Why Lord is life so fragile?

*But you have transcended death and pain*
*You have RISEN*

Help me to hold on to that promise Lord.

When I grieve
When my being feels cut in half
When I feel stunted and mutilated
When I feel severed.

Help me to hold on to that promise Lord.

When I face decisions
Without counsel
Without dialogue

Help me to hold on to that promise Lord

When I lie in bed, alone
Aching to be comforted
Longing to be caressed

When my heart is crying
and a void engulfs me

Help me to hold on to that promise Lord.

*Thank you Lord for making me aware of your presence*

I see his smile
I hear his laughter
I see him cutting the grass
and welcoming guests

221

I see my children bursting to tell him . . .
I see him listening
stroking their hair

*I know now Lord that life is eternal*

I know now Lord that you will be there to welcome me

My sadness is transformed
and gratitude has taken its place
sometimes only temporarily

My spirit is lifted and I want to sing.

You have broken through my loneliness
and have given joy back to me

You have thrown me the ball of life
that I had lost in the brambles

Thank you Lord for showing me how to live again.
Thank you Lord for helping me to reach out
not just for tit-bits
but for fullness of life.

*Barbara H. Aspell*

*There is no pain in the world, no death so sad, no grief so intense, as when a mother loses a child. For she grieves for part of her own self, her future, the wasted potential, the joyous moments of which she has been robbed, the grand-children she never saw. My own grandmother lost her only son when he was 28 and her grief was terrible and frightening. But somehow, from the depths of their beings, many women seem to be able to call upon immense reserves of strength and courage. Some, like Susan Hill, will mother again, and find new, though very different joy. Women, even though they may be worlds apart, are united in this. United too with a woman who, though she has no children of her own, discovered what it meant to mourn for a child.*

*SUSAN HILL, the writer, longed to have a second child, to complete her family. But baby Imogen was born very prematurely. She held onto the slender thread of life for five weeks, probably the longest five weeks in any mother's life. Her loss after such a fight was a severe blow, but Imogen's story nonetheless is one of the triumphs of the human spirit in pain and the deepest grief.*

We walked away slowly down the corridor and, as we went, I felt the final breaking of the cord that had bound me to her, and I remembered the Bible's words. '. . . or ever the silver cord be loosed or the golden bowl be broken . . . then shall the dust return to the earth as it was; and the spirit shall return to God who gave it.'

Going out of those doors, driving away slowly down the hospital drive, I felt as lost, as bleak and bereft and homeless as I have ever felt in my life. I didn't belong there any longer, that was over. Imogen was dead and out of reach, the baby I had never really known, but had loved more than life – she had gone. Her struggle, mine, everybody's, had been as futile as any battle in any war – the end result only pain and loss and emptiness.

At home, then, I began to cry. I had not really done so until now: I cried for her, for myself, for us all, for the waste and the anguish, her pain and bewilderment, my guilt at causing it, cried out of misery and desolation and bereavement and rage.

223

And as I cried, milk poured out of my breasts, another kind of weeping . . .

And so I went on crying, healthy, necessary tears, and I raged too, raged bitterly inside myself, against God – if he was there. After all, who had broken all his promises, led me so cleverly up the garden path, deceived me, cheated, made Imogen suffer and done nothing about it, allowed her to die? When I was alone in the house, I walked about like a wild, mad woman, like Ophelia, or the demented mother in Britten's opera *Curlew River*; I cried out her name over and over again, and I beat on the walls and into the pillows with my fists, and sometimes screamed so loudly, in such rage and pain, that I made my throat sore.

If anyone had heard me, I think I would have frightened them. They would perhaps have been seriously concerned for me, but in fact I knew instinctively, at the time, and even more now, how right and healthy it all was. Letting out grief and all the pent-up strain, by crying and shouting, expressing and releasing anger, are good and healthy things to do. They are *right* . . .

A friend who had herself lost a baby son many years before, wrote to me after Imogen's death. 'You will never ever forget her or stop loving her', she said. 'You will think of her every single day without fail, for the rest of your life. Take comfort from that.'

I have. I do.

*Susan Hill*


*CHRISTINE GARDINER is chaplain of St Christopher's Hospice in Kent.*


A small white coffin and me! For the first time in ministry as a hospital chaplain I found myself taking the funeral of a day-old baby in the absence of his parents. Sue and Paul were too hurt to come to little John's funeral having lost their first child fourteen months prior to John's birth. I was not prepared for the feelings that were to emerge when there were no parents to care for and concentrate on.

As my maternal feelings shot to the fore, I realized that I was no longer the minister, but the mother, and the funeral director seemed to metamorphose into John's father for a while, as he entered the cemetery chapel, and we stood silently together while I asked for strength from God to commend this child into the love of his heavenly Father.

We walked up to the graveside ten minutes later in a howling gale with driving rain stinging our faces. Flower petals were blowing from other graves and falling upon us like confetti. We gathered some of them and placed them on the tiny grave. 'Here John, these are for you', I whispered. And the words were followed by the sound of muffled crying, from both of us. We said goodbye with all our love, and the love of Paul and Sue. As we did so and I committed his body to the ground, a sense of peace enfolded us like a safe and quiet shelter in the midst of the storm.

Our natural maternal and paternal feelings had been used to say goodbye to John for his Mum and Dad. It felt as if human and divine love had met around that grave in a special way for a special purpose not fully known to ourselves. The experience was painful, but very beautiful, and as we walked away from our parent role across the muddy pathways, tears and raindrops still fresh on our faces, I felt God's smile and baby John's too, warm and comfort my heart. 'Lord, please let Sue and Paul feel this too', I prayed.

*Christine Gardiner*

# In Maturity

It comes to us all. That moment when we look in the mirror and see ourselves as if for the first time. We wonder where the creases came from and in shock rush out rashly for our first pot of expensive anti-wrinkle cream.

And then gradually reason takes over, and we tell ourselves that we have not been confronted with our fading female attractiveness, but rather with the signs of a new, mature identity. For wisdom and experience have drawn all kinds of interesting designs upon our faces. Love and hate, joy and bitterness, sweetness and sourness; it is written there for all to see, the choices we made, the inner attitudes which motivated us, the measure of self we have given.

Regrets there will inevitably be, a sense of loss and decay, but as Christine Gardiner puts it so vividly, dying for the Christian is only the passageway to resurrection life. In winter the tree may look barren, wizened, gnarled and unfruitful. But that is only the beginning, not the end of the story.

*MARJORIE FERARD was born at the end of the last century in Ireland amidst 'the troubles'. She subsequently married an army officer and followed him wherever he was posted, to the Himalayas, Kashmir, Afghanistan. She looks back, now that her horizons are limited by physical restrictions, with a twinkle*

*in her eye, at a life rich in colour and experience, captured in*
*the many delightful anecdotes she still tells, and in the hundred*
*or so poems she has written.*

## Regret for Youth

The years have wrapped themselves in dead, brown leaves,
And drifted down the streams of Time,
With outstretched hands I stood upon the brink,
Eager to catch them, as they swirled away,
But elfin-like they fluttered by
– Faster, and ever faster.
And now it is too late – the boughs above are bare,
Grim Winter waits – and see, how grey my hair.

*Marjorie Ferard*

## Disappointment

I thought I was immune from the mid-life crisis. Until the day
dawned when I began to think of all the books I would now
never read, all the people I would never know, the information I
would never appropriate, the adolescent aspirations which
would never be fulfilled. It's a dangerous time. A time to build
on what has been, or a time for falling prey to bitter, crushing
disappointment.

I remember my paternal grandmother as a disappointed
person. Hers had been a hard and difficult life. She came to
Britain from Latvia with her parents, sister and four brothers
as a young girl. In Latvia the professions had been closed to
the Jews. Some had become landowners, money-lenders and
businessmen, incurring wholesale Latvian resentment and
dislike. Others remained poor and became the scapegoats of

228

the long-suffering peasant folk there. Many heard of a better life for Jews on a cold, grey, little island in the middle of the North Sea and decided to take their chance. Life could be no worse than it was, that was for sure.

My four great-uncles found work quickly. But their parents couldn't settle and went back to Latvia, leaving the two daughters to clean and keep house for their four elder brothers.

Back in Eastern Europe, the middle-aged couple had two more daughters to ease their sorrow and loneliness, who grew up hearing all about their six elder brothers and sisters on the other side of Europe whom they had never met. But life was hard in Latvia. Poverty and persecution continued unabated and the old couple decided to emigrate again, to die in peace in the real land of promise, the United States of America. They chose to sail on a ship which docked en route in Southampton, so that the two younger girls could meet their six brothers and sisters for the first time, so that they could see their beloved children again for the last time.

My grandmother and her brothers were beside themselves with excitement at the thought of seeing their parents again and meeting their two younger sisters. For weeks they spoke and thought of nothing else, as they saved up the precious pennies and planned the great adventure.

At last the great day came and the six of them sat on Southampton quay in a fever of expectation. A dot appeared on the horizon and materialized slowly into a ship, coming ever closer. Suddenly it stopped and weighed anchor. They waited and watched, but it didn't move. Frantic, they hunted round for someone to ask and were informed that due to unfavourable tides, the boat would not now be docking after all.

For several hours they continued to sit on the quay, straining their eyes to catch the tiniest glimpse of someone vaguely resembling a person. They didn't even have a pair of binoculars. And they were still watching when, at last, the ship pulled away and disappeared into the distance.

Disappointment on that scale is unimaginable. 'Crushed hope makes the heart sick', says the proverb. As winter succeeds winter, as the ageing process continues unabated, and adolescent dreams and aspirations fade into the distance and vanish like the ship, I think I can identify with my grandmother's feelings a little more than when I was young.

My grandmother never saw her parents again, never recovered from that or many of the other disappointments in her life. She always left me feeling slightly depressed. In the end she took her own life.

'But . . .', the proverb continues, 'a dream come true is a tree of life.'

Unlike my grandmother, I want to go on being a dreamer. I've always believed that God plants his dreams in our hearts so that he can make them come true one day. Perhaps the adolescent aspirations need to be abandoned, the disappointments left behind, and the present lived to the full, because the mature dreams are the best. And who knows what the future holds?

The two American sisters did reappear. There were visits and reunions, and cousins who wrote and became close. And my grandmother missed it all.

*Michele Guinness*

*Irma Kurtz, the American writer, claimed on Radio 4 recently that men 'die', but women 'change'. The obituary lists are always full of men, because women have disappeared from centre stage earlier, when their reproductive systems cease to function.*

*The menopause can be seen as a kind of death, a farewell to a major part of woman's* raison d'etre, *according to many of the religious and social traditions. But for those who have eyes*

230

*to see it is the time for woman to emerge from the chrysalis of her dying body into a new stage of life. The Chinese, who venerate age for its wisdom and experience, know that only too well.*

### Menarche to Menopause

The smear test done,
As I roll off the couch
My doctor asks:
'How's the menopause?
If you've had no periods
For a year,
Count yourself free . . .'

FREE?

I go home to old diaries,
Check some dates:
Yes, it's true,
During the last year –
Nothing!

FREE?

Still half bemused
I think back, realize
It's been forty years
Since that Easter-time
While staying at an aunt's –
The sudden, urgent rush
To her scented bathroom
Where I found, drastically,
My grown-up Self had come:

231

And now I see, although
What's taken place
Is called 'The Change',
In fact the changing has been happening
Over years,
Gradually, in energies
And attitudes
Till now I stand –

FREE!

To renew acquaintance
With my Self – take up
Travel, Art, Design,
Music, and the Writing
For so long laid aside –

FREE!

Still 'Me'
But now restored,
Renewed, recharged,
Expanded . . .
Yes, I'm changed
And I emerge, readied
For this new stage in Life

*Anonymous*

*REVD MARGARET CUNDIFF went on record as saying that for her life really did begin at forty. She responded to a debate on the subject on* Woman's Hour *on Radio 4, and from that moment her media career really took off. For many years she contributed to the 'Pause for Thought' slot on Radio 2, establishing herself firmly in the nation's heart as the warm, wise, comfortable, 'Mother of the airwaves'.*

*She still serves as a non-stipendiary deacon at St James' Church in Selby, and Broadcasting Officer for the York Diocese. She has nine books and a weekly column in the* Selby Times *to her credit. Ordination to the priesthood, a dream she has held for many years, is still a possibility, but she recognizes that sixty is a rather special landmark in her life.*

## Role Reversal

It is a strange feeling being sixty. I don't feel sixty, but then what does sixty feel like? I enjoyed the party. I took the jokes, 'in good part' – or so they tell me. I managed to smile anyway. I am delighted with my bus tokens, rail card and details of concessionary fares.

But what next?

It has been creeping up on me for some years, I now realize, this 'role reversal': the children urging me to 'go carefully', fussing about me keeping my purse safe and not talking to strangers. They even offer to look after my money, but I assure them I'm not *that* old! I suppose I should stop calling them children, for they are, as I tell them, approaching middle-age themselves.

It's the first year since my mother's death and I still think of things I want to share with her, still pick up a pretty card or gift for her, and remember . . . My father, always so big and strong and determined is now a small, frail, dependent man, content for me to make decisions, to help him across the road, to give him advice. I think of the years that have passed, and see how roles reverse with age.

What next?

I want life to go on just the same as ever, the 'eternal

teenager', and yet I know time moves on. I see my friends growing older, some seem so staid, so set, so . . . old? Then I look in the mirror and see . . . what? Perhaps I would rather not see.

But there are advantages in growing older. The years have taught me lessons. I have kept old friends, and made new ones. My husband is happily adjusted to his retirement at last – it took him a long time to reach that stage. Someone said to me last week, 'You're but a lass yet. Wait until you have another twenty years under your belt', and he's a lively eighty-five. So maybe there is life after sixty!

What about God? What does he think of me at sixty?

'Do not be afraid, I will save you. I have called you by name. You are mine.'

His promise to me is as true today as it was yesterday, and will be for all my tomorrows. He is my Father and I am his child – forever. There is no role-reversal to fear with him. Whatever changes the years bring, he will not change. To him I am Margaret. Not Margaret, daughter, wife or mother; not Margaret, deacon, rail card holder, pensioner. Just Margaret. I have nothing to fear, for I am safe and secure, and always will be.

*Margaret Cundiff*

*JENNY JOSEPH was born in Birmingham in 1932 and has won many major literary awards for her collections of poetry. She read English as a scholar of St Hilda's College, Oxford, and has worked as a newspaper reporter, pub landlady and lecturer in adult education. She is now a freelance writer and lecturer.*

## Warning

When I am an old woman I shall wear purple
With a red hat which doesn't go and doesn't suit me.
And I shall spend my pension on brandy and summer
   gloves
And satin sandals, and say we've no money for butter.
I shall sit down on the pavement when I'm tired
And gobble up samples in shops and press alarm bells
And run my stick along the public railings
And make up for the sobriety of my youth.
I shall go out in my slippers in the rain
And pick the flowers in other people's gardens
And learn to spit.

You can wear terrible shirts and grow more fat
And eat three pounds of sausages at a go.
Or only bread and pickle for a week
And hoard pens and pencils and beermats and things in
   boxes.

But now we must have clothes that keep us dry
And pay our rent and not swear in the street
And set a good example for the children.
We will have friends to dinner and read the papers.

But maybe I ought to practise a little now?
So people who know me are not too surprised
When suddenly I am old and start to wear purple.

*Jenny Joseph*

*Waiting to become a grandmother for the first time can be as rich a time of anticipation as for the mother, perhaps more so, as there is no morning sickness or discomfort this time, and a certain objectivity about the whole process which allows the prospective grandma a sense of being part of some great, eternal and infinite mystery.*

## The Grandmother's Song

Hullo Hullo
You're there I know
Each day I see your mother grow
Heavier more beautiful and slow.

Deep, deep
You sleep
And stretch and swim
In secret waters
Warm and dim
Where archetypal dreams arise
And float behind your unborn eyes.

To you in there
So close so far
The dead are no more distant
Than the living are
You are a part
Of us and them
And all of us, like you

Are old and new
Intricate fragile and sublime
Waiting and growing
In the womb of time.

*Ann Morrish*

## The Grandchildren Grow Older

All down the street she pitter-patter went,
and picked her way among the snow and ice,
and peered through frosted panes, to read the price
on lace-edged handkerchiefs and Yardley's scent,

but in her heart she knew they would not do,
so to the counter bravely forged ahead,
where, after much debate, she bought instead
a wild and heady fragrance named Tabu.

Then past the Beatrix Potters, wistfully,
to where the long-range missiles were displayed,
with plastic gun, bazooka, hand grenade,
for waging war on land and air and sea

and so went laden home, with things designed,
one way or other, to undo mankind.

*Evangeline Paterson*

One day, after a month of continuously being with people in the midst of their suffering and loss, I felt I had lost all glimmer of strength and hope. I kept repeating to myself, and to God, 'What's the use? Everything hurts and everything dies!'

I decided that afternoon to put on my mac and wellingtons and go for a walk in the park. I walked through an avenue of trees as the sun came through the clouds, shining on the wonderful autumn colours. Stopping next to one particularly large oak tree I watched its leaves cascading down from its branches, leaving them bare. The wind seemed to be nothing but a thief and a robber. I meditated on the process of the loss

237

of summer glory. The tree itself appeared to be quite content and not alarmed at its loss, readily giving itself to the seemingly destructive elements of wind and rain. Slowly light dawned as God's message through his creation gently penetrated my mind and spirit.

Hidden within the tree already was the power to create the new spring bud . Resurrection hope began to return and faith was rekindled. The fact that life and death and resurrection were all part of the same mystery of our lives became clearer as I walked on across the park. I thought, 'Here I am going through the menopause. I thought my body was withering and dying as well. Now I can see that this too is a time of resurrection to the next season of life.'

As I walked on I felt almost tangibly the flow of healing within my inner self. I was recovering from a sad and busy month, from the mental adjustment to the changes in my body. But that final resurrection with its promise of new life is surely the source of hope and healing for all our lives.

*Christine Gardiner*

## 17th-Century Nun's Prayer

Lord thou knowest better than I know myself
that I am growing older and will some day be old.
Keep me from the fatal habit of thinking I must say
    something on every subject and every occasion.
Release me from craving to straighten out everybody's
    affairs. Make me thoughtful but not moody: helpful but
    not bossy.
With my vast store of wisdom,
it seems a pity not to use it all.
But thou knowest, Lord, I want a few friends at the end.

238

Keep me reasonably sweet. I do not want to be a saint –
some of them are hard to live with.
But a sour old person
is one of the crowning works of the Devil.

Keep my mind free from the recital of endless details;
give me wings to get to the point.
Seal my lips on my aches and pains.
They are increasing and love of rehearsing them
is becoming sweeter as the years go by.
I dare not ask for grace enough
to enjoy the tales of others' pains,
but help me to endure them with patience.

I dare not ask for improved memory
but for a growing humility,
and a lessening cocksureness when my memory
seems to clash with memories of others.
Teach me the glorious lesson that occasionally
I may be mistaken.

Give me the ability to see good things
in unexpected places
and talents in unexpected people.
And give me, O Lord, the grace to tell them so.

*Anonymous*
*– found in Rochester Cathedral*

*HANNAH WHITALL SMITH (1832–1911) was born to a Quaker family in Philadelphia. She was a founder member of the Women's Christian Movement and the suffrage movement in the States, wrote extensively and is well known for her best-selling classic,* The Christian's Secret of a Happy Life.

I am convinced it is a great art to know how to grow old gracefully, and I am determined to practise it . . . I always thought I should love to grow old, and I find it is even more delightful than I thought. It is so delicious to be done with things, and to feel no need any longer to concern myself much about earthly affairs . . . I am tremendously content to let one activity after another go, and to await quietly and happily the opening of the door at the end of the passageway, that will let me in to my real abiding place.

*Hannah Whitall Smith*

*This poem was written to be read by Stewart's wife, Carol, at the funeral of her best friend, her mother, written as though her mother were speaking.*

### F.M.D.

When I was a girl
cantering past sixteen
all was so bright,
even the mosquito evenings
had the lucid, luminous moon

Later, as a young mother
tugging some of my babies
past the wolf's breath of war
above Blackheath, I found
it was only a short eclipse

Then, through the giddy spring
of no more bombs
we learned new phrases
'You've never had it so good'
and discarded old ones
'Put that light out'

After all this
came the merry glow of ballgowns
skating like nimble beacons
around the candle, candelabra rooms
and all was so bright

In the stone bunting City of David
near the almond blossom tree
I learned the mysteries of
suffering and the necessary training
for my new address

Now, at the end,
bright is a small, weak word
to describe the dazzling table
at which I now feast,
the candescent palace that I inhabit
with His paschal perfume smeared on the door
But, so that you may understand,
I will say once more
Now at the end
all is so bright.

*Stewart Henderson*

*ADRIAN PLASS, the writer, is best known for his satire, his ability to send up the foibles of the Christian Church. Perhaps it is his great gift for humour which makes his serious writing all the more powerful and poignant.*

*He wrote this poem for his friend Chris, who found as he nursed his mother at the end of her earthly life, through the continual exchange of the caring and receiving roles, that their relationship deepened into something neither had anticipated or imagined.*

I mothered she who mothered me,
The body that I never knew,
(Though she knew mine so well when I was
small and she was all my need).
So plaintive now,
Her arms surrendered high to be undressed or dressed,
Like some poor sickly child,
Who sees no shame in helplessness,
Embarrassed once, but all too happy now,
To let me ease her weariness.
And yet, when I collapsed and cried beside her on the bed.
She was my mother once again,
She reached her hand out to the child in me,
She dried my tears,
And held me there till I was still.
So ill, so long
Until, at last, when endless days of hopefulness had
    faded finally
There came a night of harmony, a night of many psalms,
I mothered she who mothered me
And laid my sister gently
In our father's arms.

*Adrian Plass*

# Sources and Acknowledgements

The compiler and publishers are pleased to acknowledge the authors and publishers of the works listed below for permission to quote from their copyright material. Special thanks are also due to those contributors whose work is not mentioned here because it was either specially written for this collection or published here for the first time.

### In the Beginning

'Chauvinist Creation' by Gordon Bailey, from *Stuff and Nonsense, A Collection of Verse and Worse* (Lion 1989).
'Eve's Story', from the Quaker Journal, *The Friend*.
'Deception' by Veronica Zundel, from *Faith in Her Words, Six Centuries of Women's Poetry*, compiled by Veronica Zundel (Lion 1991).
'Counter-Balance' by Stewart Henderson, by permission of the author, from his 'Counter-Balance' roadshow.

### Girls

'The Girlchild' by Jenny Cooke, first appeared in *Childbirth – A Christian Perspective* (Grove Booklet on Ethics No 43).
'Advice to Daughters' by Evangeline Paterson, from *Bringing the Water Hyacinth to Africa* (Taxus Press 1983).
'For You are a Woman' by Zeemat Ahmed, first printed in November 1986 in a Bangladeshi women's bulletin, by permission of the translator, Mukti Barton.

**A Woman's Love**

'Walking on Water' by Ellen Wilkie, from Ellen Wilkie with Judith Gunn, *A Pocketful of Dynamite* (Hodder and Stoughton 1990), by permission of the publisher and author's family.

Letters by Grace Hurditch Guinness and 'She has come to my heart', from Michele Guinness, *The Guinness Legend* (Hodder and Stoughton 1990).

'Ex' by Ellen Wilkie, from Ellen Wilkie with Judith Gunn, *A Pocketful of Dynamite* (Hodder and Stoughton 1990).


**Marriage**

Catherine Booth on Marriage from Catherine Bramwell-Booth, *Catherine Booth* (Hodder and Stoughton 1970).

'On Choosing a Husband' by Catherine Booth, from *The Training of Children and Courtship and Marriage* (Salvationist Publishing and Supplies 1953).

'A Wife Meditates on her Beloved, From the Bathroom' by Stewart Henderson, from *A Giant's Footsteps* (Hodder and Stoughton 1989).

'Let There Be Spaces in Your Togetherness', from Kahlil Gibran, *The Prophet* (William Heinemann 1980).

'The Spectre of the Other Woman' by Joyce Huggett, from *Listening to Others* (Hodder and Stoughton 1988).

'When a Wife Becomes a Carer', from *The Book of Margery Kempe*, tr. Susan Dickman and quoted in *Medieval Women's Visionary Literature*, ed. Elizabeth Alvilda Petroff (OUP 1986).

'When the End Comes' by William Booth, from Catherine Bramwell-Booth, *Catherine Booth* (Hodder and Stoughton 1970).


**Being Single**

'The Late Bride' by Veronica Zundel, from *A Long Journey* (Marina Press 1991).

'Eternity, I'm Coming' by Emily Dickinson, from *Complete Poems*, ed. T. H. Johnson (Faber 1976).

Catherine Marshall, from *Meeting God at Every Turn* (Hodder and Stoughton 1980).

'For One-Parent Families' by Sylvia Jury, from *She Prays, A Collection of Prayers and Poems for International Women's Day, 1975*, ed. Dss Phoebe Willetts (printed privately).


**Pregnancy and Childbirth**

'I Wanted to be a Bridge' by Penelope Flint, from *All the Days of My Life* (Hodder and Stoughton 1989).

'Why Should She' by Lucy Guinness Kumm, from *From the Heart of Motherhood* (Longman, Green and Company 1929).

'The Firstborn' by Jenny Cooke, first printed in *Childbirth – a Christian Perspective.*

'Made Flesh' by Luci Shaw, from *Listen to the Green* (Harold Shaw Publishers 1971).

'The Grandchild' by Frances Mary Marston, from *What is A Baby?*, writings selected by Richard and Helen Exley (Exley Press 1980).


**On Being Mum**

A meditation by Mother Teresa, from *In the Silence of the Heart, Meditations by Mother Teresa of Calcutta*, compiled by Kathryn Spink (SPCK 1983).

Angela Ashwin, from *Heaven in Ordinary, Contemplative Prayer in Ordinary Life* (Mayhew McCrimmon 1985).

Clare Richards, from *From Nun to Mum* (Triangle 1991).

Caroline Philps, from *Mummy, Why Have I Got Down's Syndrome?* (Lion 1991).

'To My Son – and my heavenly Father' by Jane Grayshon, from *Faith in Flames* (Hodder and Stoughton 1991).

'The Love that Passes Knowledge' by Lucy Guinness Kumm, from *From the Heart of Motherhood* (Longman, Green and Company 1929).

'Our True Mother, Jesus' by Mother Julian of Norwich, from Julian of Norwich, *Revelations of Divine Love*, tr. Clifton Wolters (Penguin Classics 1966).

'Three a.m. – A Mother Waits' by Jenny Robertson, from *Faith in Her Words, Six Centuries of Women's Poetry*, compiled by Veronica Zundel (Lion 1992).
'The Mother's Blessing' from *The Carmina Gadelica*, ed. Alexander Carmichael, in six volumes (Scottish Academic Press 1971).
'Parting From My Son' by Evangeline Paterson, from *Bringing the Water Hyacinth to Africa* (Taxus Press 1983).

**Daddy's Girl**

'First Lesson' by Phyllis McGinley, from 'A Girl's Eye-View of Relatives', from *Times Three* (Sheed and Ward 1959).
'Dad' by Elaine Feinstein, from *Some Unease and Angels, Selected Poems* (Hutchinson 1977).
'Compassion' by Tracy Hansen, from *Seven for a Secret* (Triangle 1991).

**Sisters!**

'Sisters' by Hilda Cohen, from *No Holds Barred, The Raving Beauties Choose New Poems by Women* (The Women's Press 1985).

**Women and Sexuality**

'The Woman' by R. S. Thomas, from *Later Poems 1972–1982* (Macmillan 1983).
Anne Townsend, from *Faith Without Pretending* (Hodder and Stoughton 1990).
Sister Margaret Magdalen CSMV, from *Transformed by Love* (Darton, Longman and Todd 1989).
Letters of Charles and Fanny Kingsley, from *The Oxford Book of Marriage*, ed. Helge Rubinstein (OUP 1990).
'One Flesh' by Elizabeth Jennings, from *Collected Poems* (Carcanet 1986), by permission of David Higham Associates.

**A Woman's Lot**

'Christ, How Can You Know?' by Amanda Swallow, from *She Prays*, ed. Dss Phoebe Willetts (printed privately).

Lady Hosie, from 'Christ and Women' in *Women in the Pulpit*, ed. D. P. Thompson (James Clarke n.d.), quoted in *The Hidden Tradition, Women's Spiritual Writings Rediscovered*, ed. Lavinia Byrne (SPCK 1991).

Evangeline Booth, from *Women* (Fleming Revell 1930), quoted in *The Hidden Tradition*, ed. Lavinia Byrne (SPCK 1991).

Dorothy L. Sayers, from 'Are Women Human?' in *Unpopular Opinions* (Victor Gollancz 1946), by permission of David Higham Associates.

'Men and Women' by Godfrey Holmes, from *Beginning Where I Am, Meditations for Young People* (Triangle 1991).

'I am a Woman' by Gabriele Dietrich, from Chung Hyun Kyung, *Struggle to be the Sun Again, Introducing Asian Women's Theology* (SCM Press 1990).

'The Corset' by Elma Mitchell, from *People Etcetera* (Peterloo Poets 1987).

## Woman At Work

'The Teacher' by Evelyn Underhill, from *The Spiritual Life of the Teacher* (Longman, Green and Company 1934).

'Pardon my *Cri de Coeur*', first printed in the *Guardian*, 7 May 1992, as 'An Article of Lost Faith'.

'The Nurse' by Jane Grayshon, from *Faith in Flames* (Hodder and Stoughton 1991).

'The Carer' by Sheila Cassidy, from *Sharing the Darkness* (Darton, Longman and Todd 1988).

## A Woman Spurned

Dorothy L. Sayers, from 'Are Women Human?' in *Unpopular Opinions* (Victor Gollancz 1946), by permission of David Higham Associates.

'Did the Woman Say' by Frances Croake Frank, published in the *National Catholic Reporter*, 21 December 1979.

'The Hidden Sun' by Hiratsuka Raicho, first published in *Voices of Women, An Asian Anthology*, ed. Alison O'Grady (Asian Christian Women's Conference in Singapore 1978).

'One Woman's Ministry' by Sue Minton, first published in *Chrysalis*, the journal of the Movement for the Ordination of Women, January 1992.

'The Anointing' by Edwina Gateley, from *Psalms of a Laywoman* (Anthony Clarke Books 1988).

## Where Women are Powerless

'Intercessions' by Joan Pluciennik, from *She Prays*, ed. Dss Phoebe Willetts (printed privately).

'God in the Brothel' by Edwina Gateley, from *I Hear a Seed Growing* (Anthony Clarke Books 1990).

'Ain't I Woman?' by Sojourner Truth, set out by Erlene Stetson, from *Faith in Her Words*, compiled by Veronica Zundel (Lion 1991).

## Women of Courage

'I Understand' Ursula's speech, from Dorothy L. Sayers, *The Zeal of Thy House* (Camelot Press 1937), by permission of David Higham Associates.

'Mrs Lack's Cake', from David Michell, *A Boy's War* (Overseas Missionary Fellowship 1988).

Corrie Ten Boom, from *Clippings From my Notebook* (Triangle 1982).

Mary Craig, from *Blessings* (Coronet Books, Hodder and Stoughton 1979).

'I Sit on the Floor' by Irena Ratushinskaya, from *Grey is the Colour of Hope*, tr. David MacDuff (Hodder and Stoughton 1988).

Mary Stocks, from *My Commonplace Book* (Peter Davies 1970), quoted in *The Hidden Tradition*, ed. Lavinia Byrne (SPCK 1991).

'A Woman's Cry of the Heart' by Dss Phoebe Willetts, by permission of Revd Alfred Willetts.

'Endings and Beginnings' by Rosie Hopper, by permission of Richard Hopper.

## Women and Achievement

'A Litany for Many Voices' by Janet Crawford and Erice Webb, from *Celebrating Women*, ed. Janet Morley and Hannah Ward (WIT/MOW 1986).

248

Jennifer Rees Larcombe, from *Unexpected Healing* (Hodder and Stoughton 1991).

## A Woman's Brokenness

'Broken' by Jean Clark, from *Celebrating Women*, ed. Janet Morley and Hannah Ward (WIT/MOW 1986).
'Do Not Kiss Me' by Jane Grayshon, from *Faith in Flames* (Hodder and Stoughton 1991).
Catherine Marshall, from *Meeting God at Every Turn* (Hodder and Stoughton 1981).
Joyce Huggett, from *Listening to God* (Hodder and Stoughton 1986).
'In Solidarity' by Kathy Keay, from *Letters From a Solo Survivor* (Hodder and Stoughton 1991).
'New Life in the Hidden Place' by Rae Williams, first printed in *The Rite Lines*, the quarterly magazine of Broken Rites.

## Friendship

'Dear Hannah' by Kathy Keay, from *Letters From a Solo Survivor* (Hodder and Stoughton 1991).

## Women's Spirituality

Mother Maribel of Wantage, from Sister Janet CSMV, *Mother Maribel of Wantage* (SPCK 1972).
Sheila Cassidy, from *Sharing the Darkness* (Darton, Longman and Todd 1988).
Anne Townsend, from *Faith Without Pretending* (Hodder and Stoughton 1990).
Dorothy Day, from *On Pilgrimage, The Sixties* (Curtis Books 1972).
Caryll Houselander, from *The Comforting of Christ* (Sheed and Ward 1947).
Clare Richards, from *From Nun to Mum* (Triangle 1991).
Catherine Booth Clibborn, from *Our Children* (George H. Doran 1925).
'The Maypole' by Judith Pinhey, from *The Dance of Life* (Fount 1992).

'God Ran Away' by Edwina Gateley, from *I Hear a Seed Growing* (Anthony Clarke Books 1990).


## Saying Goodbye and Grieving

Michelene Wandor, from *Walking on the Water, Women Talk About Spirituality*, ed. J. Garcia and S. Maitland (Virago 1983).
Susan Hill, from *Family* (Penguin 1990).


## In Maturity

'Regret for Youth' by Marjorie Ferard, from *Amusing and A-Musing, Selected Poems* (printed privately 1982).
'Warning' by Jenny Joseph, from *Selected Poems* (Bloodaxe Books 1992), by permission of John Johnson Ltd.
'The Grandchildren Grow Older' by Evangeline Paterson, from *Lucifer at the Fair* (Taxus 1991).
Hannah Whitall Smith, from '*A Religious Rebel*', *The Letters of H. W. Smith* (1949), quoted in *Christian Faith and Practice in the Experience of the Society of Friends*, No 519 (London Yearly Meeting of the Religious Society of Friends 1960).
'F.M.D.' by Stewart Henderson, from *A Giant's Scrapbook* (Hodder and Stoughton 1989).
'I Mothered She' by Adrian Plass, from *View From a Bouncy Castle* (Fount 1991).


The compiler and publishers have made every effort to trace the copyright holders of the material here. Information on any omissions should be sent to the publishers who will make full acknowledgement in any future editions.